The Ethics of Life and Death Exploring Medical Dilemmas

Wilder Mario

Copyright © [2023]

Title: The Ethics of Life and Death Exploring Medical Dilemmas
Author's: Wilder Mario

This book was printed and published by [Publisher's: **Wilder Mario**] in [2023]

ISBN:

TABLE OF CONTENT

Chapter 3: End-of-Life Care and Euthanasia

Understanding End-of-Life Care

The Ethics of Euthanasia

Assisted Suicide: Legal and Ethical Perspectives

Palliative Care and the Ethical Dilemmas Involved

Chapter 4: Reproductive Technologies and Ethical Issues

Ethical Considerations in Assisted Reproductive Technologies

Surrogacy: Legal and Ethical Implications

Genetic Testing and Screening: Ethical Challenges

Abortion: Perspectives on Ethics and Rights

Chapter 5: Organ Transplantation and Allocation

Organ Donation: Ethical Considerations

The Allocation of Scarce Resources

Living vs. Deceased Organ Donation: Ethical Implications

Organ Trafficking and Black Market: Ethical Concerns

Chapter 6: Research Ethics and Human Subjects

Chapter 7: Global Health Ethics

Chapter 8: Emerging Technologies and Ethical Implications

Chapter 12: Conclusion and Future Directions in Medical Ethics

Recapitulation of Key Ethical Issues Explored

The Evolving Landscape of Medical Ethics

The Role of Education and Training in Ethical Decision Making

Challenges and Opportunities in Advancing Medical Ethics

Chapter 1: Introduction to Medical Ethics

Definition of Medical Ethics

Medical ethics is a branch of ethics that examines the moral principles and values that guide healthcare professionals in making decisions and providing care to patients. It encompasses a set of principles and guidelines that ensure the ethical conduct of medical practitioners and promote the well-being of patients.

At its core, medical ethics is concerned with the ethical dilemmas and challenges that arise in the field of medicine. It provides a framework for healthcare professionals to navigate complex situations and make decisions that are morally right and in the best interest of the patient.

The foundation of medical ethics lies in four key principles: autonomy, beneficence, non-maleficence, and justice. Autonomy refers to respecting the patient's right to make decisions about their own healthcare. Beneficence focuses on promoting the well-being of the patient and taking actions that benefit them. Non-maleficence emphasizes the obligation to do no harm to the patient. Lastly, justice entails treating patients fairly and equitably, ensuring equal access to healthcare resources.

Medical ethics also involves other important concepts such as confidentiality, informed consent, and the duty of care. Confidentiality ensures that patient information remains private and is not shared without their consent. Informed consent requires healthcare professionals to provide patients with all necessary information about their condition, treatment options, and potential risks so that they can make informed decisions about their care. The duty of care refers to the ethical responsibility of healthcare professionals to provide competent and compassionate care to their patients.

Ethical dilemmas are common in medical practice, and medical ethics helps professionals navigate these challenges. These dilemmas may include issues such as end-of-life care, organ transplantation, genetic testing, and resource allocation. Medical ethics provides a framework for evaluating these dilemmas, weighing the benefits and risks, and making decisions that are ethically sound.

In conclusion, medical ethics serves as a moral compass for healthcare professionals, guiding their actions and decisions in the best interest of their patients. It ensures that patients are treated with respect, dignity, and fairness while upholding the core principles of autonomy, beneficence, non-maleficence, and justice. By understanding and adhering to the principles of medical ethics, healthcare professionals can navigate the complex ethical landscape of medicine and provide compassionate and ethical care to their patients.

Importance of Medical Ethics in Society

Medical ethics play a crucial role in shaping the moral fabric of society. In a world where medical advancements are rapidly progressing, it becomes imperative to have a set of guidelines and principles that govern the practice of medicine. "The Ethics of Life and Death: Exploring Medical Dilemmas" aims to shed light on the significance of medical ethics, addressing a wide audience including individuals from all walks of life, particularly those interested in the field of ethics.

At its core, medical ethics ensures that healthcare professionals adhere to moral and ethical standards while providing medical care. It lays the foundation for compassionate and responsible healthcare practices, emphasizing the importance of respect, honesty, and integrity in the doctor-patient relationship. This subchapter delves into the various dimensions of medical ethics and their impact on society.

Firstly, medical ethics safeguards the rights and dignity of patients. It recognizes the autonomy of individuals, ensuring that they have the right to make informed decisions about their own healthcare. By promoting patient-centered care, medical ethics fosters trust between patients and healthcare providers, resulting in better health outcomes and improved patient satisfaction.

Secondly, medical ethics serves as a framework for addressing complex moral dilemmas. It equips healthcare professionals with the tools to navigate challenging situations, such as end-of-life decisions, organ transplantation, and resource allocation. By engaging in ethical decision-making, healthcare providers can ensure that the best interests of their patients are always prioritized, even in ethically ambiguous circumstances.

Furthermore, medical ethics promotes social justice and equality in healthcare. It emphasizes the importance of fair distribution of healthcare resources, ensuring that vulnerable populations are not marginalized or excluded from essential medical care. By advocating for equitable access to healthcare services, medical ethics contributes to a more just and inclusive society.

In conclusion, the importance of medical ethics in society cannot be overstated. It sets the standards for ethical conduct in medicine, protecting the rights and dignity of patients, guiding healthcare professionals in complex situations, and promoting social justice in healthcare. "The Ethics of Life and Death: Exploring Medical Dilemmas" invites readers from all backgrounds, particularly those interested in ethics, to delve deeper into the significance of medical ethics and its impact on society. By understanding and upholding medical ethics, we can ensure that healthcare remains a noble profession, dedicated to the well-being of individuals and the betterment of society as a whole.

Historical Background of Medical Ethics

In order to fully understand the ethical dilemmas that modern medicine faces, it is essential to explore the historical background of medical ethics. The evolution of medical ethics has been shaped by various cultural, religious, and philosophical beliefs throughout history. By delving into the past, we can gain valuable insights into the principles that guide medical practice today.

One of the earliest recorded codes of medical ethics can be found in the Hippocratic Oath, attributed to the ancient Greek physician Hippocrates. This oath, which dates back to the 5th century BCE, emphasized the importance of the physician's duty to prioritize the well-being of their patients above all else. It also established guidelines against performing certain procedures, such as abortion and euthanasia.

Throughout the medieval period, medical ethics were heavily influenced by religious doctrines, particularly those of Christianity. The concept of the sanctity of life emerged during this time, emphasizing that human life is sacred and should be preserved at all costs. Medical practitioners were expected to adhere to these principles, even if it meant refraining from potentially life-saving procedures.

The Enlightenment era brought about a shift in medical ethics, as rational thinking and scientific advancements began to challenge traditional beliefs. The work of philosophers such as Immanuel Kant and John Stuart Mill paved the way for the development of ethical theories like deontology and utilitarianism, respectively. These theories sought to establish a more systematic approach to medical ethics, focusing on the consequences of actions and the principles that guide them.

The 20th century witnessed significant milestones in medical ethics. The Nuremberg Code, established after the atrocities committed by Nazi physicians during World War II, laid the foundation for ethical research involving human subjects. The Declaration of Helsinki, later adopted by the World Medical Association, provided further guidelines for medical research ethics.

In recent decades, medical ethics has been shaped by advancements in technology and the growing influence of patient autonomy. Concepts such as informed consent, patient confidentiality, and end-of-life decision-making have gained prominence, empowering individuals to actively participate in their own healthcare.

Understanding the historical background of medical ethics helps us appreciate the challenges faced by healthcare professionals and society as a whole. By recognizing the diverse influences that have shaped medical ethics over time, we can engage in thoughtful discussions and make informed decisions regarding the ethical dilemmas that arise in the field of medicine. Ultimately, this knowledge enables us to navigate the complex landscape of medical ethics with compassion, integrity, and respect for human life.

Ethical Principles in Medical Practice

Introduction:

In the field of medicine, ethical principles serve as a compass that guides healthcare professionals to make decisions and provide care that is both morally and socially responsible. These principles are rooted in the values of beneficence, non-maleficence, autonomy, and justice. This subchapter aims to explore the significance of ethical principles in medical practice, shedding light on their impact on patient care and the larger society.

1. Beneficence:

Beneficence refers to the ethical obligation of healthcare professionals to act in the best interest of their patients. It emphasizes the importance of promoting well-being, preventing harm, and providing optimal care. This principle underscores the need for physicians to prioritize the patient's needs, ensuring that their actions lead to positive outcomes.

2. Non-Maleficence:

Linked closely with beneficence, non-maleficence emphasizes the duty to do no harm. Medical practitioners must avoid actions that may cause unnecessary harm or suffering to patients. This principle compels physicians to carefully weigh the potential risks and benefits of medical interventions, always striving to minimize harm.

3. Autonomy:

Respecting patient autonomy is a fundamental principle in medical ethics. It recognizes an individual's right to make informed decisions about their own healthcare. Healthcare professionals must provide patients with comprehensive information, allowing them to make choices that align with their values and preferences. Informed consent is a crucial aspect of ensuring patient autonomy.

4. Justice:

Justice in medical practice refers to the fair distribution of healthcare resources, benefits, and burdens. This principle calls for equal access to healthcare, regardless of factors such as socioeconomic status, race, or gender. It also encompasses healthcare professionals' responsibility to advocate for equitable healthcare policies and challenge systemic disparities.

Conclusion:

By adhering to ethical principles, healthcare professionals can navigate complex medical dilemmas while upholding the highest standards of care. Beneficence, non-maleficence, autonomy, and justice form the foundation of ethical medical practice, promoting patient welfare, respecting individual rights, and striving for fairness. Understanding and applying these principles is crucial for all healthcare providers, as they shape the delivery of healthcare and the relationships between medical professionals and patients. Ultimately, ethical medical practice is not only essential for individual patients but also for creating a just and compassionate society.

Chapter 2: Autonomy and Informed Consent

The Principle of Autonomy

In the realm of medical ethics, the principle of autonomy holds great significance. It is a fundamental concept that emphasizes the respect for an individual's ability to make informed decisions about their own lives, particularly in the context of medical treatment and end-of-life choices. This principle recognizes that every person has the right to govern their own body and make decisions that align with their values, beliefs, and personal circumstances.

Autonomy is a principle that applies to all individuals, regardless of age, gender, or cultural background. It asserts that each person has the capacity and freedom to make choices that affect their health and well-being. In the medical field, this principle guides healthcare professionals to obtain informed consent from patients before initiating any treatment or procedure. It ensures that patients are fully aware of the risks, benefits, and alternatives available to them, allowing them to make decisions that reflect their own values and goals.

Moreover, the principle of autonomy also extends to end-of-life choices, such as advance directives and euthanasia. It recognizes that individuals have the right to make decisions regarding their own death, especially when faced with terminal illness or unbearable suffering. These choices should be respected and supported, enabling individuals to have a dignified and compassionate end to their lives.

However, the principle of autonomy is not absolute and can be limited by certain factors. For instance, if a person lacks decision-making capacity due to severe cognitive impairment or mental illness, their autonomy may be compromised. In such cases, healthcare professionals and family members may need to make decisions on their behalf, guided by the person's previously expressed wishes or best interests.

It is important for every individual, regardless of their background, to understand and appreciate the principle of autonomy. By doing so, they can actively participate in their own healthcare decisions, ensuring their voices are heard and respected. Furthermore, healthcare professionals and policymakers must also be mindful of this principle, ensuring that they provide the necessary information and support to empower individuals in making autonomous choices.

Ultimately, the principle of autonomy is a cornerstone of medical ethics. It upholds the inherent right of every individual to make decisions about their own bodies and lives, fostering a culture of respect, dignity, and patient-centered care. By embracing this principle, we can navigate the complex ethical dilemmas that arise in the medical field and strive towards a more compassionate and patient-centric healthcare system.

The Role of Informed Consent in Medical Decision Making

In the realm of medical ethics, few concepts hold as much importance as informed consent. It is a foundational principle that guides medical professionals and patients alike in making crucial decisions about healthcare treatments and interventions. In this subchapter, we will explore the critical role of informed consent in medical decision making and its ethical implications.

At its core, informed consent refers to the process by which patients are provided with all the necessary information about their medical condition, potential treatments, risks, and benefits. This enables them to make autonomous decisions based on their values, preferences, and understanding of the situation. Informed consent is essential for upholding patient autonomy and ensuring that individuals have the right to make decisions about their own bodies and health.

From an ethical standpoint, informed consent is a manifestation of respect for persons. It recognizes the inherent dignity and worth of each individual and acknowledges their right to participate in decisions that impact their well-being. Informed consent seeks to empower patients by providing them with the knowledge necessary to actively engage in their healthcare, fostering a collaborative doctor-patient relationship.

Informed consent also serves as a safeguard against potential abuses in medical practice. It protects patients from unwanted or unnecessary treatments, ensuring that they have the opportunity to weigh the risks and benefits of proposed interventions. Moreover, it prevents paternalistic attitudes that disregard an individual's right to autonomy and self-determination.

However, achieving truly informed consent is not always straightforward. Factors such as language barriers, limited health literacy, power imbalances, and time constraints can hinder the process. Medical professionals must strive to communicate effectively and ensure that patients have a genuine understanding of the information provided. This requires presenting information in a clear and accessible manner, addressing any questions or concerns, and allowing sufficient time for deliberation.

Informed consent is not a one-time event but rather an ongoing process that evolves as new information becomes available or as a patient's circumstances change. It requires continuous communication, trust, and shared decision-making between patients and healthcare providers. By embracing the principles of informed consent, we can promote patient autonomy, foster ethical medical practices, and ultimately prioritize the well-being of all individuals.

In conclusion, informed consent plays a vital role in medical decision making and is an essential component of ethical healthcare. It upholds patient autonomy, protects against potential abuses, and fosters collaborative doctor-patient relationships. By recognizing the importance of informed consent and striving to ensure its implementation, we can navigate the complex terrain of medical dilemmas with compassion, respect, and ethical integrity.

Challenges in Obtaining Informed Consent

In the complex world of medicine, the concept of informed consent plays a pivotal role in ensuring ethical decision-making and patient autonomy. Informed consent is a fundamental principle that enables patients to make informed choices about their healthcare. However, it is not without its challenges. This subchapter delves into the intricacies and difficulties surrounding the process of obtaining informed consent.

One of the primary challenges in obtaining informed consent lies in the complexity of medical information. Healthcare professionals often struggle to convey complex medical jargon to patients in a manner that is easily understandable. The technical language used in medical discussions can be overwhelming for individuals without a medical background. This challenge is further exacerbated when dealing with patients who have low health literacy levels or those who belong to marginalized communities. Bridging this communication gap is essential to ensure that patients fully comprehend the risks, benefits, and alternatives of their proposed treatment options.

Another issue that arises in obtaining informed consent is the power dynamics between healthcare professionals and patients. Patients may feel intimidated or fearful of questioning their healthcare providers, leading to a power imbalance that hinders the true essence of informed consent. It is crucial for healthcare professionals to foster an environment of open dialogue and encourage patients to voice any concerns or doubts they may have. Additionally, healthcare providers must be mindful of their own biases and beliefs to ensure that patients are receiving unbiased information.

In some cases, emergencies or time constraints may make it challenging to obtain informed consent. Life-threatening situations or urgent medical interventions necessitate swift decision-making, leaving little time for detailed discussions with patients or their families. Balancing the need for immediate action with the principles of informed consent can be a delicate task for healthcare professionals.

Furthermore, cultural and religious beliefs often influence a person's decision-making process, posing additional challenges in obtaining informed consent. Healthcare providers must be sensitive to these factors and strive to accommodate diverse perspectives and values. Respectful dialogue and cultural competency training can help healthcare professionals navigate these challenges effectively.

In conclusion, obtaining informed consent is essential in upholding patient autonomy and ethical decision-making in the field of medicine. However, various challenges exist that must be addressed for the process to be truly effective. Bridging the communication gap, addressing power dynamics, considering time constraints, and respecting cultural and religious beliefs are crucial steps in ensuring that patients can make informed choices about their healthcare. By acknowledging and addressing these challenges, healthcare professionals can strive towards a more patient-centered approach, promoting the principles of ethics in the realm of life and death decisions.

Ethical Considerations in Autonomy and Informed Consent

In the field of medicine, the concepts of autonomy and informed consent are of utmost importance. They form the foundation for ethical decision-making and ensure that patients are treated with respect and dignity. This subchapter delves into the ethical considerations surrounding autonomy and informed consent, exploring their significance in medical dilemmas.

Autonomy, in the context of healthcare, refers to an individual's right to make decisions about their own medical care. It recognizes that patients have the right to choose what happens to their bodies, based on their own values and beliefs. Respecting patient autonomy means involving them in the decision-making process and providing them with complete and accurate information about their condition, treatment options, potential risks, and benefits.

Informed consent is the process through which patients are provided with relevant information to make autonomous decisions about their healthcare. It is not merely a formality but an ethical obligation of healthcare providers. Informed consent requires that patients understand the nature of their condition, the proposed treatment, alternative options, potential risks, and expected outcomes. They should also be made aware of any potential conflicts of interest that may influence their healthcare decisions.

However, ethical dilemmas can arise when patients lack the capacity to make autonomous decisions due to cognitive impairments, mental illness, or age-related issues. In such cases, the principles of beneficence and non-maleficence come into play. Healthcare providers must act in the best interest of the patient, while also considering their values and wishes.

Additionally, cultural and religious beliefs may impact a patient's decision-making process. Ethical considerations demand that healthcare professionals respect and accommodate these beliefs, as long as they do not contradict established medical guidelines or cause harm to the patient.

Moreover, confidentiality and privacy play a crucial role in maintaining patient autonomy. Healthcare providers must ensure that patient information is kept confidential, unless there are compelling reasons to share it. This ensures that patients feel safe and comfortable sharing sensitive information, enabling them to make informed decisions without fear of judgment or discrimination.

In conclusion, ethical considerations in autonomy and informed consent are vital to maintaining patient-centered care. Respecting patient autonomy, providing informed consent, considering the best interests of the patient, and accommodating cultural and religious beliefs are all essential aspects of ethical decision-making in healthcare. By upholding these principles, healthcare providers can enhance trust, foster collaboration, and ensure the well-being of their patients.

Chapter 3: End-of-Life Care and Euthanasia

Understanding End-of-Life Care

End-of-life care is a crucial aspect of healthcare that requires a deep understanding of both medical practices and ethical principles. It involves providing support and medical treatment to patients who are approaching the end of their lives, with the aim of ensuring their comfort and dignity during this difficult time. This subchapter aims to provide a comprehensive understanding of end-of-life care, exploring the ethical considerations that come into play and the various approaches to delivering compassionate and effective care.

One of the key ethical considerations in end-of-life care is the principle of autonomy, which recognizes an individual's right to make decisions about their own healthcare. This principle is particularly important when it comes to decisions regarding life-sustaining treatments, such as artificial ventilation or resuscitation. Understanding a patient's wishes and respecting their autonomy is essential in providing appropriate end-of-life care.

Another important ethical principle is beneficence, which focuses on promoting the well-being of the patient. In end-of-life care, this principle guides healthcare professionals in providing pain management, symptom control, and emotional support. It also emphasizes the importance of effective communication with patients and their families, ensuring that their needs and desires are addressed throughout the care process.

End-of-life care can take various forms, depending on the patient's condition and preferences. Hospice care, for example, focuses on providing comfort and support to patients with terminal illnesses.

Palliative care, on the other hand, can be provided alongside curative treatments and aims to improve the patient's quality of life by managing pain and other distressing symptoms.

Additionally, advance care planning plays a significant role in end-of-life care. It involves discussing and documenting a patient's preferences for medical treatment in the event that they become unable to make decisions for themselves. This includes decisions about resuscitation, use of life-sustaining treatments, and preferences for comfort care. Discussing these topics early on ensures that the patient's wishes are respected and can alleviate the burden on family members who may otherwise have to make difficult decisions on their behalf.

Understanding end-of-life care is vital for everyone, as it not only affects patients but also their families and healthcare professionals. It requires a delicate balance between medical expertise and ethical considerations. By recognizing the principles of autonomy and beneficence, exploring different care approaches such as hospice and palliative care, and engaging in advance care planning, we can ensure that end-of-life care is provided with compassion, respect, and dignity. This subchapter aims to equip readers with the knowledge and understanding necessary to navigate the complexities of end-of-life care ethically and effectively.

The Ethics of Euthanasia

Introduction:

Euthanasia, derived from the Greek words "eu" meaning good and "thanatos" meaning death, is a topic that elicits strong emotions and impassioned debates. It involves the deliberate act of ending a person's life to relieve their suffering from a terminal illness or an incurable condition. The ethical dimensions surrounding euthanasia are complex, as they delve into questions of autonomy, compassion, dignity, and the sanctity of life. In this subchapter, we will explore the various ethical arguments surrounding euthanasia and attempt to shed light on this contentious issue.

Autonomy and Compassion:

Proponents of euthanasia argue that it is an exercise of autonomy, allowing individuals to decide the manner and timing of their own death. They believe that it is a compassionate act that can alleviate immense suffering, offering a merciful release from pain and indignity. Supporters emphasize that patients with terminal illnesses should have the right to end their lives with dignity, rather than endure prolonged suffering.

Sanctity of Life:

Opponents of euthanasia, however, contend that life is inherently sacred and that intentionally ending it is morally wrong. They argue that the sanctity of life should be protected at all costs, and that euthanasia undermines this fundamental principle. These individuals often advocate for palliative care and the improvement of end-of-life services as alternatives to euthanasia.

Slippery Slope:

One of the ethical concerns associated with euthanasia is the potential for a slippery slope, whereby legalized euthanasia may lead to abuse and the devaluation of vulnerable lives. Critics fear that if euthanasia becomes acceptable, it could be expanded beyond terminally ill patients to include those with chronic illnesses, disabilities, or even those who are simply tired of life. Such a scenario raises significant ethical questions about the potential for discrimination and the erosion of societal values.

Legal and Ethical Considerations:

The legal status of euthanasia varies across different countries and jurisdictions. While some nations have legalized euthanasia or physician-assisted suicide under specific circumstances, others strictly prohibit it. These divergent approaches reflect the ongoing ethical debate surrounding the practice.

Conclusion:

The ethics of euthanasia are multifaceted and deeply rooted in personal beliefs, cultural values, and philosophical perspectives. As advancements in medical science continue to extend human life, the ethical dilemmas surrounding end-of-life decisions become increasingly relevant. By examining the arguments for and against euthanasia, we can engage in informed discussions and decision-making processes that respect both individual autonomy and the sanctity of life. Ultimately, it is crucial to find a balance that safeguards human dignity, compassion, and the preservation of ethical values in the face of life's most challenging circumstances.

Assisted Suicide: Legal and Ethical Perspectives

Introduction:

In today's society, the topic of assisted suicide sparks intense debates surrounding both its legality and ethical implications. The act of intentionally helping someone end their life raises profound questions about the value of life, personal autonomy, and the role of medical professionals. This subchapter aims to explore the legal and ethical perspectives surrounding assisted suicide, providing a comprehensive understanding to a diverse audience interested in ethics.

Legal Perspectives:

The legality of assisted suicide varies across different countries and states, reflecting the diverse cultural and moral values held by societies. Some jurisdictions categorically reject assisted suicide as illegal, while others have implemented legislation to allow it under specific circumstances. This subchapter will explore the legislative frameworks in place, discussing landmark cases that have shaped the legal landscape and analyzing the arguments surrounding the right to die.

Ethical Perspectives:

Assisted suicide poses complex ethical dilemmas, challenging individuals to navigate conflicting values and beliefs. From a deontological standpoint, the sanctity of life is seen as an absolute, making any form of intentional harm or killing morally impermissible. On the other hand, consequentialist perspectives may argue that assisted suicide can alleviate suffering and respect individual autonomy, promoting the greatest overall happiness. This subchapter will delve into these ethical frameworks, examining the arguments for and against assisted suicide, and addressing the potential consequences on patients, families, and medical professionals.

The Role of Medical Professionals:

The involvement of medical professionals in assisted suicide raises unique ethical considerations. Physicians, who have sworn to preserve life and alleviate suffering, find themselves at the intersection of patient autonomy and professional responsibility. This subchapter will explore the ethical challenges faced by doctors, nurses, and other healthcare providers, discussing the impact of assisted suicide on the doctor-patient relationship, medical ethics, and the broader healthcare system.

Conclusion:

Assisted suicide remains a highly controversial and emotionally charged topic, eliciting strong reactions from individuals across all walks of life. This subchapter aimed to provide a comprehensive analysis of the legal and ethical perspectives surrounding assisted suicide, offering a nuanced understanding of this complex issue. By exploring the diverse viewpoints and considering the implications for medical professionals and patients, we hope to foster informed discussions and encourage critical thinking on this sensitive topic. Ultimately, it is up to society to engage in thoughtful dialogue and carefully consider the legal and ethical ramifications of assisted suicide, in order to arrive at a collective understanding that best serves the needs and values of individuals in our diverse and ever-evolving world.

Palliative Care and the Ethical Dilemmas Involved

In the realm of medicine, the field of palliative care stands as a beacon of hope and compassion for those facing life-limiting illnesses. This specialized branch of healthcare focuses on providing relief from pain and symptoms, as well as addressing the emotional, psychological, and spiritual needs of patients and their families. However, as with any complex medical endeavor, palliative care presents its own set of ethical dilemmas that demand careful consideration.

One of the primary ethical dilemmas in palliative care revolves around the administration of pain medication, particularly opioids. While these drugs are highly effective in managing pain, there is a fine line between adequate pain relief and the risk of addiction or overdose. Healthcare providers must grapple with the balance between ensuring patients' comfort and ensuring their safety, often in the face of conflicting desires of patients, family members, and legal regulations. Striking the right balance requires a thorough understanding of the patient's medical condition, their wishes, and an ongoing evaluation of their pain management needs.

Another ethical dilemma in palliative care centers around the withdrawal or withholding of life-sustaining treatments. When faced with terminally ill patients who have no hope of recovery or whose treatment options are limited, healthcare professionals must consider whether it is ethical to continue interventions that may only prolong suffering. This decision-making process involves a delicate interplay of respecting patient autonomy, ensuring the provision of comfort and dignity, and adhering to legal and ethical guidelines.

Furthermore, the ethical challenges extend to end-of-life decision-making and advance care planning. Palliative care teams often find themselves assisting patients in making difficult decisions regarding life-sustaining treatments, resuscitation orders, and the use of interventions such as feeding tubes or ventilators. Encouraging open and honest communication and facilitating shared decision-making between patients, their families, and healthcare providers becomes paramount in ensuring that patient preferences and values are honored.

Ultimately, palliative care is a complex and multifaceted field that necessitates ethical awareness and sensitivity. It requires healthcare professionals to navigate the delicate balance between providing comfort and respecting autonomy, all while adhering to legal and ethical frameworks. By acknowledging and actively engaging with the ethical dilemmas inherent in palliative care, we can strive to deliver the highest standard of care to patients and their families, ensuring that their journey through life's final stages is characterized by compassion, dignity, and respect.

Chapter 4: Reproductive Technologies and Ethical Issues

Ethical Considerations in Assisted Reproductive Technologies

Assisted reproductive technologies (ART) have revolutionized the field of reproductive medicine, offering hope to couples struggling with infertility and enabling individuals to have biological children where it was previously impossible. However, the ethical implications of these technologies are complex and multifaceted. In this subchapter, we will explore the ethical considerations surrounding ART and the dilemmas they pose.

One of the primary ethical concerns in ART is the issue of autonomy and consent. While individuals have the right to make decisions about their reproductive choices, the use of ART often involves third parties, such as sperm or egg donors, gestational carriers, or surrogate mothers. Questions arise regarding the extent to which these individuals can give informed consent and the potential exploitation that may occur in these arrangements.

Another significant ethical consideration is the potential for the commodification of human life. The commercialization of ART raises concerns about the exploitation of vulnerable individuals, especially in countries with lax regulations. The sale of gametes, embryos, or surrogacy services can lead to the exploitation of individuals from disadvantaged backgrounds and may reduce the value of human life to a mere transaction.

Furthermore, the use of ART presents challenges in the realm of genetic selection and manipulation. Technologies like preimplantation genetic diagnosis (PGD) allow for the screening of embryos for genetic disorders, but they also open the door to selecting embryos for non-medical traits. The concept of "designer babies" raises ethical questions about eugenics and the potential for creating a society that values certain traits over others.

The emotional and psychological implications of ART should also be considered. While the desire to have a child is understandable, the pursuit of parenthood through ART can be emotionally taxing and financially burdensome. The psychological well-being of individuals and couples undergoing ART, as well as the potential impact on children conceived through these technologies, must be carefully considered.

In conclusion, assisted reproductive technologies offer immense possibilities for individuals and couples facing reproductive challenges. However, the ethical considerations surrounding these technologies cannot be ignored. Autonomy, commodification, genetic selection, and emotional well-being are all ethical concerns that must be carefully weighed when considering the use of ART. It is crucial to strike a balance between the potential benefits of these technologies and the ethical principles that guide our understanding of human dignity, justice, and the value of life.

Surrogacy: Legal and Ethical Implications

Surrogacy is a complex and controversial topic that raises numerous legal and ethical questions. In recent years, advancements in reproductive technologies have made surrogacy a viable option for couples struggling with infertility or same-sex couples aiming to start a family. However, the practice of surrogacy is not without its challenges, with legal and ethical implications that demand careful consideration.

From a legal standpoint, surrogacy laws vary greatly across different countries and even within regions. Some countries prohibit commercial surrogacy altogether, while others allow it under certain conditions. These variations in legal frameworks give rise to a multitude of issues, such as determining the rights and responsibilities of intended parents, surrogates, and the child. Additionally, the potential for exploitation of surrogates in countries where regulations are lax or non-existent is a significant concern.

Ethically, surrogacy raises questions about the commodification of reproduction and the potential exploitation of vulnerable individuals. Critics argue that commercial surrogacy turns the process of creating life into a transaction, where money is exchanged for the use of a woman's body. This perspective raises concerns about the potential for surrogates to be coerced or forced into the arrangement due to economic circumstances.

Another ethical dilemma arises when considering the emotional and psychological impact on all parties involved. Surrogates may experience a range of emotions, from attachment to the fetus they carry to potential grief upon relinquishing the child. Intended parents may face challenges in developing a bond with a child biologically unrelated to them. The well-being of the child also becomes a crucial ethical consideration, as questions about their rights, identity, and the circumstances surrounding their conception and birth arise.

To navigate these legal and ethical implications, it is essential to establish a comprehensive and balanced regulatory framework that protects the rights and well-being of all parties involved. This framework should prioritize the autonomy and agency of surrogates while ensuring that the best interests of the child are upheld. It must also address the potential for exploitation and ensure that individuals are not coerced into participating in surrogacy arrangements.

Surrogacy is a complex and multifaceted topic that requires careful examination from legal and ethical perspectives. The moral implications of commercial surrogacy, the rights of all parties involved, and the potential for exploitation demand thoughtful consideration. As society continues to grapple with these issues, it is crucial to engage in open and informed dialogue to establish ethical guidelines that protect the dignity and well-being of all individuals involved in the surrogacy process.

Genetic Testing and Screening: Ethical Challenges

In recent years, advancements in genetic testing and screening have opened up a myriad of possibilities in the field of medicine. These techniques allow us to analyze an individual's genetic makeup and identify potential risks for certain diseases or conditions. While this has undoubtedly brought about numerous benefits, it has also raised a host of ethical challenges that must be carefully considered.

One of the primary ethical concerns surrounding genetic testing and screening is the issue of privacy and confidentiality. When individuals undergo genetic testing, they are essentially revealing highly personal and sensitive information about themselves and their families. Questions arise regarding who should have access to this information and how it should be safeguarded. Should insurance companies or employers be allowed to use genetic information to make decisions about coverage or employment? Striking a balance between the need for privacy and the potential benefits of sharing genetic data is a crucial ethical challenge.

Another ethical dilemma arises in the realm of reproductive genetic testing. Prenatal genetic testing allows prospective parents to identify any genetic abnormalities in their unborn child. While this may provide them with valuable information and the opportunity to make informed decisions, it raises questions about the value and sanctity of human life. Should parents have the right to terminate a pregnancy based on genetic test results? The ethical implications of such decisions are complex and often deeply personal.

Furthermore, genetic testing and screening can also lead to unintended consequences, such as genetic discrimination. If individuals are found to have a higher risk for certain diseases, they may face discrimination in various aspects of life, including employment or obtaining insurance. This raises concerns about fairness and justice, as individuals should not be penalized or treated differently based on their genetic makeup.

Additionally, the rapid advancement of genetic technology raises questions about the potential misuse of this information. Genetic engineering and gene editing techniques have the potential to alter the course of human evolution. Ethical considerations must be made regarding the boundaries of genetic manipulation and the potential consequences of playing with the human genome.

In conclusion, genetic testing and screening present us with incredible opportunities for early detection and prevention of diseases. However, they also pose significant ethical challenges that cannot be ignored. Striking a balance between privacy and sharing of genetic information, addressing reproductive dilemmas, preventing genetic discrimination, and setting limits on genetic manipulation are all crucial considerations. As we navigate the ethical landscape of genetic testing, it is essential for society as a whole to engage in thoughtful and informed discussions to ensure that we make decisions that are fair, just, and respectful of the sanctity of life.

Abortion: Perspectives on Ethics and Rights

Introduction:

In modern society, few topics evoke as much controversy and passionate debate as abortion. The issue of terminating a pregnancy raises complex ethical and moral questions that intersect with personal beliefs, religious values, and individual rights. This subchapter aims to delve into the multifaceted perspectives on the ethics and rights surrounding abortion, providing a comprehensive overview to foster a deeper understanding.

1. The Sanctity of Life: One perspective often cited in discussions on abortion is the belief in the sanctity of life. Advocates argue that life begins at conception and that every embryo or fetus possesses inherent value and the right to life. This viewpoint places a strong emphasis on the protection of unborn life, often arguing that abortion is morally equivalent to murder.

2. Women's Autonomy and Reproductive Rights: Conversely, another perspective focuses on women's autonomy and reproductive rights. Proponents of this view argue that a woman has the right to make decisions about her own body, including the choice to terminate a pregnancy. They assert that restrictions on abortion infringe upon women's fundamental rights, such as bodily autonomy and the right to privacy.

3. Moral Status of the Unborn: The question of when personhood or moral status begins is central to the abortion debate. Some argue that personhood begins at conception, while others propose that it begins at viability or birth.

This debate raises questions about the rights and moral status of the unborn, and whether they should be considered as individuals with inherent rights.

4. Utilitarian Considerations: Utilitarian ethics introduce a different angle to the abortion debate by focusing on the consequences of actions. Supporters of this perspective argue that the decision to have an abortion should be based on factors such as the woman's well-being, the potential quality of life for the child, and the overall societal impact. They contend that abortion can be ethically justified if it minimizes harm and maximizes overall happiness.

5. Cultural, Religious, and Legal Variations: Abortion debates are further complicated by cultural, religious, and legal variations across different nations and communities. This subchapter will explore some of the diverse perspectives and practices worldwide, ranging from countries with restrictive abortion laws to those where access to safe and legal abortion is readily available.

Conclusion:

The issue of abortion remains a deeply divisive topic, with ethical considerations and individual rights at the forefront of the debate. By exploring the various perspectives outlined in this subchapter, readers can gain a more nuanced understanding of the complex factors that shape opinions on abortion. Ultimately, the aim is to encourage respectful dialogue and foster a society where individuals can engage in meaningful discussions about this contentious issue.

Chapter 5: Organ Transplantation and Allocation

Organ Donation: Ethical Considerations

Organ donation is a complex and morally challenging topic that raises numerous ethical considerations. It involves the voluntary transfer of organs from one individual to another, often to save or improve the recipient's life. While organ transplantation has become a crucial medical procedure, its ethical implications cannot be overlooked.

One of the key ethical concerns surrounding organ donation is the issue of consent. The decision to donate organs, whether it be while alive or after death, should always be based on informed consent. It is essential to ensure that potential donors fully understand the risks, benefits, and consequences of organ donation. Furthermore, consent should be voluntary, free from coercion or undue influence. Respecting an individual's autonomy and right to make decisions about their own bodies is paramount.

Equitable distribution is another ethical consideration. The demand for organs far exceeds the supply, resulting in long waiting lists and, unfortunately, deaths while waiting for a transplant. Allocating organs fairly and justly is essential to ensure that those in need have an equal opportunity to receive a transplant. Factors such as medical urgency, waiting time, and likelihood of success are typically taken into account. However, challenges arise when determining who should be prioritized and how to balance these factors ethically.

The issue of organ trafficking and commercialization is a significant ethical concern. It is important to prevent the exploitation and commodification of organs, as well as the vulnerable individuals who may be coerced or forced into donating. The sale of organs raises ethical questions about the value and dignity of human life, as well as potential exploitation of those in desperate situations. Striking a balance between increasing the organ supply and preventing unethical practices is crucial.

Religious and cultural beliefs also play a significant role in shaping ethical perspectives on organ donation. Some religions and cultures may have specific views on the body, death, and the afterlife, which can impact individuals' decisions regarding organ donation. It is essential to respect and accommodate these diverse beliefs while promoting informed decision-making.

In conclusion, organ donation raises numerous ethical considerations that require careful examination and consideration. Consent, equitable distribution, prevention of trafficking, and respect for religious and cultural beliefs are just a few of the ethical issues that must be addressed. Having open and informed discussions about these considerations is crucial to ensure that organ donation practices align with ethical principles and uphold the values of compassion, fairness, and respect for human dignity.

The Allocation of Scarce Resources

In the field of medicine, one of the most pressing ethical dilemmas is the allocation of scarce resources. As medical advancements continue to extend the boundaries of what is possible, the demand for these limited resources increases exponentially. This subchapter aims to delve into the ethical considerations surrounding the allocation of scarce resources in healthcare and shed light on the complex decisions that need to be made.

When resources such as organs for transplantation, life-saving medications, or intensive care beds are limited, difficult choices have to be made. These decisions raise fundamental ethical questions, such as who should have access to these resources, and on what basis should they be allocated? The answers to these questions have far-reaching consequences for individuals, families, and society as a whole.

One of the most common ethical frameworks used to guide resource allocation decisions is utilitarianism. Utilitarianism posits that the morally right action is the one that maximizes overall happiness or well-being. In the context of scarce resources, this may involve prioritizing those who have a higher likelihood of survival or the potential to contribute more to society.

However, utilitarianism has its critics. Some argue that it fails to adequately account for the intrinsic value of each individual life, potentially leading to the neglect of vulnerable populations or perpetuating existing social inequalities. This has led to the development of alternative ethical approaches, such as the principles of justice and fairness.

Justice and fairness demand that resources be allocated in a manner that is equitable and impartial. This means considering factors such as need, urgency, and the principle of equal opportunity. By prioritizing those with the greatest need or providing equal access to limited resources, these principles seek to ensure a fair distribution that is not solely based on maximizing overall utility.

The COVID-19 pandemic has further highlighted the ethical challenges of resource allocation. With overwhelmed healthcare systems and a scarcity of critical care beds and ventilators, healthcare professionals have been forced to make agonizing choices. The allocation guidelines implemented during this crisis have sparked debates about ageism, disability bias, and the value of life.

In conclusion, the allocation of scarce resources in healthcare is a complex and ethically charged issue. Balancing the principles of utilitarianism, justice, and fairness requires careful consideration and deliberation. As individuals and as a society, we must grapple with these dilemmas and strive to find solutions that are both morally justifiable and compassionate. Only through open dialogue and a shared commitment to ethical decision-making can we navigate the challenging terrain of allocating scarce resources in the pursuit of better health outcomes for all.

Living vs. Deceased Organ Donation: Ethical Implications

Organ transplantation has revolutionized modern medicine, offering hope and extending the lives of countless individuals suffering from organ failure. However, this medical breakthrough also raises ethical dilemmas that require careful consideration. One such dilemma is the choice between living and deceased organ donation. This subchapter explores the ethical implications associated with both types of organ donation, aiming to shed light on this complex and sensitive topic.

Living organ donation involves the voluntary donation of a healthy organ, such as a kidney or part of the liver, by a living individual. This act of selflessness can save lives and alleviate the suffering of those in need. However, concerns arise regarding the potential risks and long-term consequences for the donor. Ethical questions arise concerning the autonomy and well-being of the donor, as well as the potential for coercion or exploitation. It is crucial to strike a balance between promoting the gift of life and protecting the rights and welfare of the living donors.

On the other hand, deceased organ donation relies on the generosity of individuals who have passed away, either through natural causes or tragic accidents. This form of donation offers a unique opportunity to save multiple lives by transplanting organs such as the heart, lungs, liver, and kidneys. However, ethical considerations arise regarding the determination of death and the process of obtaining consent from the deceased or their family. Ensuring transparent and fair allocation of organs, as well as respecting the wishes of the deceased, is of utmost importance.

This subchapter also discusses the ethical implications of the scarcity of donated organs. With a limited supply of organs available for transplantation, challenging decisions must be made regarding the allocation of these life-saving resources. Ethical frameworks such as utilitarianism, justice, and fairness are examined, highlighting the ethical principles that should guide organ allocation policies.

Ultimately, this subchapter aims to prompt critical reflection and informed discussions about the ethical implications of living and deceased organ donation. It encourages readers to consider the values and principles that should inform decisions about organ transplantation and to engage in a broader conversation about the ethical dimensions of medical practices. By exploring these dilemmas, we can strive towards a more ethical and compassionate approach to the gift of life.

Organ Trafficking and Black Market: Ethical Concerns

In today's world, medical advancements have made it possible to save countless lives through organ transplantation. However, the increasing demand for organs has given rise to a disturbing phenomenon: organ trafficking and the black market. This subchapter delves into the ethical concerns surrounding this illicit trade, shedding light on the dark side of the medical community.

Organ trafficking refers to the illegal trade of organs, where organs are bought and sold on the black market. This underground market exploits the vulnerability of the poor and desperate, who are often coerced or deceived into selling their organs. This raises several ethical concerns that demand our attention and action.

Firstly, the commodification of organs raises questions about the intrinsic value of human life. When organs are treated as mere commodities, the dignity and sanctity of life are compromised. Every individual has a fundamental right to bodily integrity, and organ trafficking violates this right by reducing humans to objects of profit.

Moreover, the lack of regulations and oversight in the black market organ trade poses significant risks to both donors and recipients. Organ brokers often operate in unsanitary conditions, compromising the safety of the organ and the health of the recipient. Furthermore, the desperation of those involved in organ trafficking leads to a disregard for medical compatibility, resulting in higher rates of organ rejection and potential harm to recipients.

Another ethical concern relates to the fairness and equity of organ allocation. The black market thrives because of the scarcity of organs in the legal transplantation system. This means that those who can afford to pay exorbitant prices have greater access to life-saving organs, while others languish on waiting lists, hoping for a chance at survival. This disparity in access to organs perpetuates existing social and economic inequalities and undermines the principle of justice in healthcare.

To address these ethical concerns, it is crucial to combat organ trafficking through a multi-faceted approach. Strengthening legislation and enforcing strict penalties for those involved in the illegal organ trade is a necessary step. Additionally, increasing public awareness about the dangers and ethical implications of organ trafficking can help deter potential buyers and sellers.

Furthermore, the promotion of ethical organ donation practices and the establishment of transparent organ allocation systems can help alleviate the demand for black market organs. Encouraging individuals to become registered organ donors and implementing initiatives to increase deceased organ donation rates are vital steps towards reducing the need for illicit organs.

Organ trafficking and the black market represent an ethical dilemma that requires urgent attention. By understanding the ethical concerns associated with this underground trade and taking appropriate measures to combat it, we can strive towards a more just and equitable healthcare system that upholds the dignity and value of every human life.

Chapter 6: Research Ethics and Human Subjects

The Importance of Research Ethics

In the realm of medical sciences, research plays a pivotal role in advancing our understanding of diseases, developing new treatments, and improving overall healthcare. However, the pursuit of scientific knowledge must be conducted with a strong ethical framework to ensure that the rights and well-being of individuals are protected. This subchapter aims to shed light on the significance of research ethics in the field of medicine and the broader implications it has on society.

Ethics serves as the moral compass guiding researchers to conduct their work with integrity, honesty, and respect for human rights. It ensures that the potential benefits of research outweigh any potential harm and that the participants' autonomy and dignity are upheld. Research ethics also involves transparency in reporting findings, preventing conflicts of interest, and maintaining confidentiality. These principles are not only critical for the credibility and integrity of the scientific community but also for building public trust in medical research.

One of the primary reasons why research ethics is crucial is the protection of human subjects. The development of medical treatments and interventions often requires human trials, and it is essential to prioritize the well-being and safety of those involved. Ethical guidelines provide a framework for informed consent, ensuring that participants have a thorough understanding of the research process, potential risks, and benefits before making an informed decision to participate.

Furthermore, research ethics plays a vital role in addressing power imbalances between researchers and participants. It ensures that vulnerable populations, such as children, prisoners, or individuals with limited decision-making capacity, are not exploited or coerced into participating in studies that might not be in their best interest. By upholding research ethics, we create a more equitable and just healthcare system that respects the rights and autonomy of all individuals.

Research ethics also has broader societal implications. It promotes the responsible use of resources and prevents wastage of time, money, and effort in pursuing unethical or poorly designed studies. By adhering to ethical principles, researchers can avoid unnecessary harm, potential legal consequences, and damage to their professional reputation.

In conclusion, research ethics is of paramount importance in the field of medicine. It is the foundation upon which scientific progress is made while ensuring the protection of human subjects and upholding the principles of autonomy, dignity, and justice. By understanding and embracing research ethics, we can advance medical knowledge and improve healthcare in a manner that is both scientifically rigorous and morally sound.

Informed Consent in Research Studies

Research studies play a crucial role in advancing medical knowledge and improving patient care. However, the ethical implications surrounding the involvement of human subjects in these studies cannot be overlooked. Informed consent serves as a fundamental principle that ensures the protection of participants' autonomy, dignity, and rights. This subchapter will delve into the concept of informed consent in research studies, exploring its significance, components, and the ethical considerations associated with it.

Informed consent is a process that involves obtaining voluntary, informed, and competent agreement from individuals who are willing to participate in research studies. It requires researchers to provide detailed information about the purpose, procedures, potential risks and benefits, and alternative options of the study to the prospective participants. Additionally, participants should have a clear understanding of their right to withdraw from the study at any time without any negative consequences. Informed consent should be given freely, without any coercion or manipulation. It is a crucial aspect of research ethics, as it upholds the principles of respect for autonomy and individual dignity.

The components of informed consent include disclosure, understanding, voluntariness, and competence. Disclosure involves providing comprehensive information to participants, ensuring they receive all relevant details about the study. Understanding refers to the participants' ability to comprehend the information provided, including the purpose, procedures, risks, and benefits associated with the research. Voluntariness ensures that participants are not coerced or influenced into participating, and that they have the freedom to make an autonomous decision. Lastly, competence refers to the participants' ability to understand the information and make a rational decision.

Ethical considerations surrounding informed consent in research studies are numerous. Researchers must ensure that potential participants have the capacity to provide informed consent, particularly when vulnerable populations, such as children or individuals with cognitive impairments, are involved. Special care should be taken to obtain informed consent from these individuals, involving appropriate surrogate decision-makers or using simplified language to ensure comprehension. Researchers must also consider cultural and language barriers that may hinder the participants' understanding of the study. Additionally, the ongoing process of informed consent should be maintained throughout the study, with participants receiving updates regarding any changes in the research protocol.

In conclusion, informed consent is a vital component of research ethics, ensuring that individuals involved in research studies are fully informed and willingly participate. It serves as a safeguard, protecting participants' autonomy, dignity, and rights. Researchers must adhere to the principles of disclosure, understanding, voluntariness, and competence when obtaining informed consent. Ethical considerations, such as the capacity to provide consent and cultural barriers, must also be addressed. By upholding the principles of informed consent, research studies can maintain their integrity and promote ethical conduct in the pursuit of medical knowledge and advancements.

Ethical Issues in Clinical Trials

Introduction:

Clinical trials are essential for advancing medical knowledge and developing new treatments for various health conditions. However, conducting these trials raises several ethical concerns that must be addressed to ensure the well-being and rights of the participants. This subchapter will explore the ethical issues surrounding clinical trials, emphasizing the importance of ethical considerations in medical research.

Informed Consent:

One of the primary ethical considerations in clinical trials is obtaining informed consent from participants. Informed consent ensures that potential participants understand the purpose, risks, and benefits of the trial before voluntarily agreeing to participate. This practice respects their autonomy and protects them from potential harm. Ethical guidelines require researchers to provide comprehensive information in a language and format that participants can understand, allowing them to make informed decisions about their involvement in the study.

Vulnerable Populations:

Another critical ethical issue in clinical trials is the inclusion of vulnerable populations, such as children, pregnant women, and individuals with cognitive impairments. Extra precautions must be taken to protect these groups as they may have limited decision-making capacity or be more susceptible to harm. Ethical guidelines demand that researchers justify the involvement of vulnerable populations, ensure their safety, and obtain additional consent from guardians or legal representatives.

Conflict of Interest:

Conflict of interest is another ethical concern in clinical trials. Researchers or sponsors who have a financial stake in the outcome of a trial may be tempted to manipulate results, jeopardizing the integrity of the study. To address this issue, ethical guidelines require transparency and disclosure of any potential conflicts of interest. Independent review boards play a crucial role in ensuring the integrity of clinical trials by monitoring the study's design, execution, and reporting.

Data and Safety Monitoring:

Ethical guidelines also emphasize the importance of data and safety monitoring during clinical trials. Regular reviews of the data collected allow researchers to assess participant safety, treatment efficacy, and the trial's overall progress. Monitoring committees ensure that trials are stopped if participants are exposed to unacceptable risks or if the treatment proves to be significantly effective, thus preventing unnecessary harm or withholding of beneficial interventions.

Conclusion:

Ethical issues in clinical trials are of paramount importance to protect the rights and well-being of participants, maintain the integrity of the research, and ensure the advancement of medical knowledge. Informed consent, the inclusion of vulnerable populations, managing conflicts of interest, and robust data and safety monitoring are key considerations in upholding ethical standards in clinical research. By addressing these issues, we can promote trust, transparency, and fairness in medical research, ultimately benefiting society as a whole.

The Role of Institutional Review Boards

In the realm of medical research and experimentation, ethical considerations play a crucial role in ensuring the protection of human subjects. One of the key mechanisms in place to oversee and regulate these ethical considerations is the Institutional Review Board (IRB). This subchapter aims to shed light on the vital role played by IRBs in upholding ethical standards in medical research.

An IRB is an independent committee comprised of experts from various fields, including healthcare professionals, researchers, ethicists, and community representatives. Its primary purpose is to review, approve, and monitor research protocols to safeguard the rights and welfare of human participants. IRBs operate on the fundamental principle that every individual involved in a research project should be treated with dignity, respect, and fairness.

The responsibilities of an IRB are multifaceted. Firstly, it ensures that the risks to participants are minimized and justified by the potential benefits of the research. This includes careful examination of the study design, the informed consent process, and the protection of vulnerable populations such as children, pregnant women, and prisoners. IRBs also scrutinize the qualifications and expertise of the researchers to ensure they meet the necessary ethical standards.

Furthermore, IRBs play a crucial role in promoting transparency and accountability in medical research. They review and approve the informed consent documents, ensuring that potential participants are provided with clear and understandable information about the study, its risks, and benefits. This allows individuals to make informed decisions about their participation, empowering them to exercise their autonomy.

IRBs also monitor the progress of ongoing research, conducting periodic reviews to ensure that ethical standards are continuously maintained. They have the authority to suspend or terminate studies if they find evidence of unethical practices, non-compliance with regulations, or unforeseen risks to participants.

By providing oversight and guidance, IRBs contribute to the advancement of ethical medical research. They bridge the gap between the scientific community and the general public by ensuring that ethical principles are upheld and that research serves the best interests of society as a whole.

In conclusion, the role of Institutional Review Boards in the realm of medical research ethics is paramount. Their oversight and guidance protect the rights and welfare of human participants, promote transparency, and ensure that the scientific community upholds the highest ethical standards. By recognizing the importance of IRBs, we can foster a culture of ethical research that values the dignity and well-being of every individual involved.

Chapter 7: Global Health Ethics

Health Disparities and Inequities

In the modern world, the field of medicine has made remarkable advancements, leading to improved health outcomes for many individuals. However, while medical progress has been significant, it is essential to acknowledge the existence of health disparities and inequities that persist in our society. These disparities, rooted in social, economic, and cultural factors, create significant ethical dilemmas that must be addressed.

Health disparities refer to the differences in health outcomes and access to healthcare services among different populations. These disparities are often seen along lines of race, ethnicity, socioeconomic status, gender, and geographical location. It is crucial to recognize that these disparities are not merely a result of individual choices or genetic factors but are deeply intertwined with social determinants of health, such as education, income, housing, and healthcare access.

The existence of health disparities raises profound ethical concerns. In a just society, everyone should have equal opportunities to lead a healthy life. However, when certain populations face barriers in access to quality healthcare, they are more likely to suffer from untreated illnesses, poorer health outcomes, and a reduced quality of life. This inequality challenges our ethical duty to ensure fairness and justice in the distribution of healthcare resources.

Addressing health disparities requires a multifaceted approach. It involves not only improving access to healthcare services but also addressing the underlying social determinants of health. This may include advocating for policies that promote affordable housing, equal education opportunities, and income equality. Additionally, healthcare providers must be aware of their own biases and strive to provide culturally competent care to all patients, regardless of their background.

Furthermore, health disparities extend beyond national borders. Global health inequities exist between countries with varying levels of economic development, healthcare infrastructure, and access to resources. As a global community, we must confront these disparities and work towards securing health as a universal human right.

In conclusion, health disparities and inequities pose significant ethical challenges. To create a more just society, it is essential to recognize and address these disparities. By promoting equal access to healthcare services, addressing social determinants of health, and advocating for global health equity, we can strive towards a world where everyone has an equal opportunity to lead a healthy life.

Ethical Dilemmas in Access to Healthcare

In today's world, access to healthcare is a pressing issue that raises several ethical dilemmas. The availability and affordability of healthcare services have a significant impact on individuals' well-being and quality of life. However, the unequal distribution of healthcare resources often creates ethical challenges that need to be addressed.

One of the primary ethical dilemmas in access to healthcare is the issue of limited resources. Healthcare systems, particularly in developing countries, struggle to meet the growing demand for medical services due to limited funding and resources. This scarcity leads to difficult decisions about who should receive care and who should be prioritized. Should the limited resources be allocated based on the severity of the condition, the patient's age, or the likelihood of successful treatment? These questions raise ethical concerns as they involve weighing the value of one person's life against another.

Another ethical dilemma revolves around the concept of fairness and justice in healthcare access. In many societies, there are disparities in healthcare access based on socioeconomic status, race, or geographic location. This raises concerns about social justice and the ethical obligation to ensure equal access to healthcare for all individuals, regardless of their background. Should individuals with more financial resources have better access to healthcare than those with limited means? Is it ethically justifiable to have healthcare facilities concentrated in urban areas while neglecting rural communities?

The issue of healthcare rationing further exacerbates ethical dilemmas. When resources are scarce, healthcare providers may be forced to make difficult decisions about who receives certain treatments or interventions. These decisions can be based on factors such as the cost-effectiveness of the treatment or the potential for a positive outcome. However, these rationing decisions may raise ethical concerns regarding the value of human life and the potential for discrimination or bias in the decision-making process.

Furthermore, the ethical dilemmas in access to healthcare extend beyond national borders. Global health disparities highlight the challenges faced by individuals in developing countries who lack access to basic healthcare services. The ethical question arises as to what extent wealthier nations should provide resources and assistance to ensure equitable access to healthcare worldwide.

Addressing these ethical dilemmas in access to healthcare requires a comprehensive and collaborative approach. Policymakers, healthcare providers, and society as a whole must engage in open and transparent discussions to develop ethical frameworks that prioritize fairness, equity, and social justice. By promoting universal access to healthcare, investing in healthcare infrastructure, and addressing socioeconomic disparities, we can work towards a more ethical healthcare system that ensures the well-being of all individuals.

In conclusion, the ethical dilemmas surrounding access to healthcare are complex and multifaceted. They involve navigating issues of resource scarcity, fairness, justice, and global health disparities. By recognizing and addressing these ethical challenges, we can strive towards a healthcare system that provides equal opportunities for everyone, regardless of their circumstances.

Medical Tourism: Ethical Considerations

In recent years, the concept of medical tourism has gained significant popularity, with an increasing number of individuals seeking healthcare services abroad. Medical tourism refers to the act of traveling to another country to receive medical treatment, often at a lower cost or with shorter waiting times. While this practice may seem appealing to many, it is essential to consider the ethical implications associated with it.

One of the primary ethical considerations in medical tourism is the disparity in healthcare standards and quality across different countries. While some countries may offer world-class medical facilities and highly skilled healthcare professionals, others may have inadequate infrastructure and less stringent regulations. Patients opting for medical tourism must thoroughly research the destination country's healthcare system and ensure that they will receive the same level of care they would expect at home.

Another ethical concern is the potential exploitation of vulnerable populations in less developed countries. In some cases, medical tourists may unknowingly contribute to the exploitation of local communities by supporting facilities that do not adhere to proper ethical guidelines. It is crucial for individuals considering medical tourism to ensure that they are not inadvertently participating in activities that exploit local resources or labor.

Furthermore, the dilemma of resource allocation arises when individuals from wealthier countries seek medical treatment in countries with limited healthcare resources. This influx of medical tourists can strain the local healthcare system, diverting resources away from the local population and creating inequities in access to care. This raises questions about the fairness and justice of medical tourism and whether it perpetuates global healthcare disparities.

Informed consent is another critical ethical consideration in medical tourism. Patients must have access to accurate and comprehensive information about the risks, benefits, and alternatives of the proposed treatment. Language and cultural barriers can complicate the consent process, making it essential for medical tourists to ensure that they fully understand the potential consequences of their decisions.

Lastly, there are concerns about post-treatment care and follow-up. Medical tourists often return home shortly after their treatment, making it challenging for them to access adequate follow-up care or address any complications that may arise. This lack of continuity of care can be detrimental to the patient's health and raises ethical questions about the responsibility of healthcare providers in the destination country.

In conclusion, while medical tourism offers potential benefits, it is essential to consider the ethical implications associated with this practice. Patients must carefully weigh the potential risks and benefits, ensuring that they are not contributing to the exploitation of vulnerable populations or perpetuating global healthcare disparities. Ethical considerations such as informed consent, resource allocation, and continuity of care should guide the decision-making process for anyone considering medical tourism. Only by approaching medical tourism with a critical ethical lens can we strive to create a more just and equitable healthcare system for all.

Global Health Initiatives: Ethical Challenges

In recent decades, global health initiatives have gained significant attention as a means to address various health issues and disparities around the world. These initiatives aim to improve health outcomes, reduce disease burden, and promote the well-being of individuals across different nations. However, as these initiatives strive to achieve their noble goals, they often face numerous ethical challenges that must be carefully considered and navigated.

One of the primary ethical challenges in global health initiatives is the issue of resource allocation. Limited resources, including financial, human, and technological resources, pose a significant constraint in providing equal access to healthcare services. The allocation of these resources raises questions about fairness, justice, and prioritization. How should limited resources be distributed among different populations and regions with varying health needs? Should the focus be on acute diseases or preventive measures? These ethical dilemmas require careful consideration to ensure that the most vulnerable populations receive the necessary support and care.

Another ethical challenge lies in the potential for cultural insensitivity or imposition. Global health initiatives often involve interventions and practices that may clash with local cultural beliefs, norms, and values. Respect for cultural diversity and understanding local contexts is crucial to avoid imposing interventions that might be seen as unethical or disrespectful. Balancing the need for evidence-based practices with cultural sensitivity is essential in maintaining the ethical integrity of these initiatives.

Furthermore, global health initiatives face challenges related to power dynamics and collaboration. These initiatives typically involve collaborations between different stakeholders, including governments, non-governmental organizations, healthcare professionals, and communities. Power imbalances and unequal partnerships can undermine the ethical principles of autonomy, respect, and justice. Ensuring meaningful and inclusive collaboration is vital in addressing these ethical challenges and promoting sustainable solutions.

Lastly, global health initiatives must grapple with the question of sustainability. Short-term interventions might produce immediate positive outcomes, but long-term sustainability requires addressing underlying structural factors that contribute to poor health outcomes. This necessitates a broader focus on social determinants of health, such as poverty, education, and gender inequality. Ethical considerations involve not only providing immediate healthcare but also advocating for systemic changes that promote health equity and social justice.

In conclusion, global health initiatives are instrumental in addressing health disparities and promoting well-being on a global scale. However, they also face ethical challenges that must be carefully addressed to ensure their effectiveness and maintain ethical integrity. Allocating resources fairly, respecting cultural diversity, fostering inclusive collaborations, and promoting long-term sustainability are crucial in navigating these ethical challenges and achieving positive outcomes for all individuals and communities worldwide.

Chapter 8: Emerging Technologies and Ethical Implications

Artificial Intelligence in Medicine: Ethical Concerns

Introduction:

In recent years, the integration of artificial intelligence (AI) into the field of medicine has revolutionized healthcare practices, offering tremendous potential for improving patient outcomes, enhancing diagnosis accuracy, and streamlining treatment plans. However, alongside these promising advancements, ethical concerns surrounding AI in medicine have emerged. This subchapter aims to explore some of the key ethical considerations associated with the use of AI in medicine, addressing the concerns that impact us all.

Patient   Autonomy:

One of the primary ethical concerns involves the potential infringement on patient autonomy. As AI algorithms become increasingly proficient at diagnosing and recommending treatment options, there is a risk that patients may be deprived of their right to make informed decisions about their own healthcare. The question arises: to what extent should AI systems be allowed to influence medical decisions, and how can we ensure that patients remain active participants in their own care?

Data   Privacy   and   Security:

Another ethical concern associated with AI in medicine is the protection of patient data privacy and security. With the vast amount of personal health information collected and analyzed by AI systems, there is a heightened risk of data breaches and unauthorized access. It is crucial to establish robust safeguards to protect patient confidentiality and maintain trust between patients and healthcare providers.

Bias and Discrimination: AI algorithms are only as reliable and unbiased as the data they are trained on. Without careful attention, AI systems can perpetuate existing biases and discrimination in healthcare. For instance, if historically biased data is used to train AI algorithms, it may inadvertently lead to racial or gender disparities in diagnosis and treatment recommendations. Ethical considerations demand that AI systems be designed and monitored to ensure fairness and avoid exacerbating existing social inequalities.

Accountability and Transparency: As AI systems become more complex and sophisticated, it becomes increasingly difficult to understand the reasoning behind their decisions. This lack of transparency raises concerns regarding accountability in medical practice. Physicians and healthcare providers must be able to explain and justify the decisions made by AI systems to patients, regulators, and other stakeholders. Ensuring transparency in AI algorithms is essential to maintain trust and accountability in the medical field.

Conclusion:
Artificial intelligence has the potential to transform healthcare, improving patient outcomes and revolutionizing medical practices. However, ethical concerns surrounding AI in medicine cannot be ignored. Patient autonomy, data privacy and security, bias and discrimination, and accountability are just a few of the many ethical considerations that need to be addressed to ensure the responsible and ethical integration of AI in medicine. As technology continues to

advance, it is crucial for healthcare professionals, policymakers, and society as a whole to engage in ongoing dialogue to shape ethical guidelines and safeguard the best interests of patients.

Gene Editing: Ethical Considerations

In recent years, the field of gene editing has made significant advancements, raising numerous ethical considerations that society must grapple with. Gene editing refers to the ability to modify the DNA of living organisms, including humans, with the potential to eliminate genetic diseases, enhance desired traits, and even create genetically modified organisms. As we delve deeper into the realm of gene editing, it becomes crucial to explore the ethical implications associated with this powerful technology.

One of the primary ethical concerns surrounding gene editing is the potential for unintended consequences. While gene editing holds immense promise for curing genetic diseases, the long-term effects of altering an individual's DNA are still largely unknown. Genetic modifications in one generation can be inherited by future generations, potentially leading to irreversible changes in the gene pool. This raises questions about our responsibility to future generations and the potential risks we may be subjecting them to by meddling with the genetic code.

Another ethical consideration lies in the potential for gene editing to exacerbate existing inequalities. The technology could result in a divide between those who can afford genetic enhancements and those who cannot, creating a two-tiered society based on genetic advantages. This raises concerns about social justice and the impact on individuals who may be left behind due to their inability to access or afford gene editing treatments.

Furthermore, gene editing raises ethical questions surrounding the concept of human identity and the distinction between therapy and enhancement. While curing genetic diseases is widely seen as a beneficial application of gene editing, the notion of enhancing desirable traits raises concerns about altering the fundamental nature of what it means to be human. The line between treating an illness and enhancing abilities becomes blurred, forcing us to confront the ethical boundaries of tampering with our genetic blueprint.

Lastly, the ethical considerations of gene editing extend beyond humans to include the environment and other species. The potential creation of genetically modified organisms can have far-reaching consequences on ecosystems and biodiversity. It becomes crucial to assess the potential risks and benefits of gene editing not only for human well-being but also for the wider natural world.

As we navigate the uncharted territory of gene editing, it is crucial that we engage in a thoughtful and inclusive dialogue about the ethical considerations at stake. Society must collectively grapple with questions of unintended consequences, social justice, human identity, and the impact on the environment. By addressing these complex ethical dilemmas, we can ensure that the promising advancements in gene editing are harnessed responsibly and for the greater good of humanity and the world we inhabit.

Telemedicine and Ethical Issues in Remote Healthcare

The advent of telemedicine has revolutionized the field of healthcare, enabling healthcare providers to remotely diagnose, treat, and monitor patients using telecommunications technology. This innovative approach has expanded access to medical care, particularly for those living in rural or underserved areas. However, as with any technological advancement, telemedicine raises ethical concerns that must be carefully considered.

One of the primary ethical issues surrounding telemedicine is the potential for a lack of personal connection between healthcare providers and patients. In traditional healthcare settings, physicians develop a rapport with their patients, building trust and understanding. In remote healthcare, this personal connection is often lacking, which can have implications for the quality of care provided. Patients may feel less comfortable sharing sensitive information or may not receive the same level of empathy and support as they would during face-to-face consultations. Ethical guidelines must be established to ensure that healthcare providers maintain a compassionate and patient-centered approach in remote healthcare settings.

Another ethical concern relates to patient privacy and data security. Telemedicine involves the transmission of sensitive medical information over digital platforms, which can be vulnerable to hacking or unauthorized access. Ensuring the confidentiality and integrity of patient data is crucial and requires the implementation of robust security measures. Ethical guidelines should address issues such as informed consent for data transmission and storage, as well as protocols for handling data breaches.

Furthermore, telemedicine raises questions about the equitable distribution of healthcare resources. While it has the potential to bridge the gap between rural and urban healthcare, there is a risk that it may exacerbate existing healthcare disparities. Limited access to reliable internet connections and technological devices can hinder marginalized communities from benefiting from telemedicine services. Ethical considerations should focus on ensuring equal access to telemedicine for all individuals, regardless of socioeconomic status or geographical location.

Ethics in telemedicine also extend to the appropriate use of technology. Healthcare providers must be trained to use telemedicine platforms effectively and responsibly, ensuring accurate diagnoses, appropriate treatment plans, and appropriate follow-up care. There is a need for ethical guidelines that outline the qualifications and training requirements for healthcare professionals engaging in remote healthcare practices.

In conclusion, telemedicine offers great promise in expanding access to healthcare, but it also presents ethical challenges that must be addressed. Establishing clear guidelines and regulations is essential to ensure patient-centered care, protect patient privacy, promote equitable access to healthcare, and ensure the responsible use of technology. By navigating these ethical issues, telemedicine can truly revolutionize healthcare delivery and improve the well-being of individuals across society.

Robotics in Healthcare: Ethical Challenges

In recent years, the field of robotics has made significant advancements and has found its way into various industries, including healthcare. The integration of robotics into healthcare systems has the potential to revolutionize the way medical procedures are conducted and patient care is delivered. However, with these advancements come a myriad of ethical challenges that need to be carefully considered and addressed.

One of the primary ethical concerns surrounding robotics in healthcare is the potential for dehumanization. As robots become increasingly involved in patient care, there is a risk of diminishing the human connection between healthcare professionals and patients. Patients might feel neglected or alienated if they are treated solely by machines, devoid of the compassionate touch that only humans can provide. It is crucial to strike a balance between the efficiency and precision offered by robots and the empathetic care that humans can offer.

Another ethical dilemma arises from the question of accountability. When robots are involved in medical procedures or decision-making processes, who is responsible if something goes wrong? Determining liability in such cases can be challenging, especially if there is a failure in the technology or an error in programming. It is essential to establish clear guidelines and legal frameworks to ensure accountability and protect the rights of patients.

Privacy and data security are also significant concerns when it comes to robotics in healthcare. With the collection and analysis of vast amounts of personal health data, there is a risk of unauthorized access or misuse. Safeguarding patient information and ensuring consent and transparency in data collection are paramount to maintaining trust and upholding ethical standards.

Additionally, the economic impact of robotics in healthcare raises ethical questions regarding access and affordability. While the integration of robotics can enhance medical services, it also has the potential to widen the gap between those who can afford cutting-edge technologies and those who cannot. Ensuring equitable access to robotic healthcare solutions is crucial to prevent further disparities in healthcare delivery.

Ethical considerations are vital in shaping the future of robotics in healthcare. By engaging in thoughtful discussions and involving diverse stakeholders, we can navigate these challenges and harness the full potential of robotics while upholding the highest ethical standards. It is essential for healthcare professionals, policymakers, and society as a whole to collaborate and develop guidelines that prioritize patient well-being, protect privacy, and promote equitable access to advanced healthcare technologies. Only through such collective efforts can we truly reap the benefits of robotics in healthcare while preserving the core principles of ethics and humanity in medicine.

Chapter 9: Professionalism and Ethical Responsibilities

The Physician-Patient Relationship

The physician-patient relationship is at the heart of medical practice. It is a unique connection built on trust, respect, and a shared goal of promoting health and well-being. This subchapter explores the ethical considerations surrounding this crucial relationship, shedding light on the responsibilities of both the physician and the patient.

First and foremost, it is essential to acknowledge that the physician-patient relationship is a partnership. The physician brings medical knowledge and expertise, while the patient contributes their personal experiences, values, and concerns. This collaboration is critical in ensuring that the best possible medical decisions are made, taking into account both the clinical evidence and the patient's individual circumstances.

One ethical principle that underpins the physician-patient relationship is autonomy. Autonomy recognizes the patient's right to make decisions about their own health, including the right to refuse medical treatment. However, this autonomy is not absolute, as it must be balanced with the physician's duty to provide appropriate care and act in the patient's best interest. This delicate balance requires open and honest communication between the physician and the patient, fostering a relationship built on mutual understanding and trust.

Another important aspect of the physician-patient relationship is confidentiality. Patients must feel safe and secure in sharing sensitive information with their healthcare provider. Physicians, in turn, have a moral and legal obligation to protect their patients' privacy and maintain confidentiality. This trust is crucial in establishing a therapeutic environment where patients can openly express their concerns and fears without fear of judgment or discrimination.

The physician's duty of beneficence, or acting in the patient's best interest, is also a key ethical consideration. This duty requires physicians to weigh the potential benefits and harms of various treatment options and recommend the most appropriate course of action. However, it is important to remember that what may be considered in the patient's best interest may vary depending on individual values, cultural backgrounds, and personal beliefs.

In conclusion, the physician-patient relationship is a vital component of medical ethics. It encompasses principles such as autonomy, confidentiality, and beneficence, all of which contribute to the ethical practice of medicine. By fostering open communication, trust, and respect, healthcare providers can establish strong relationships with their patients, ultimately leading to better healthcare outcomes. This subchapter serves as a reminder of the importance of this relationship and the ethical responsibilities it entails for both physicians and patients.

Ethical Obligations of Healthcare Providers

In the ever-evolving field of healthcare, ethical considerations play a pivotal role in ensuring the well-being of patients and upholding the integrity of the healthcare profession. Healthcare providers, be it doctors, nurses, or other medical professionals, are entrusted with the responsibility of safeguarding the lives and dignity of their patients. This subchapter aims to explore the ethical obligations that healthcare providers must adhere to in their practice, thereby shedding light on the crucial intersection of ethics and healthcare.

First and foremost, one of the primary ethical obligations of healthcare providers is the principle of beneficence. This principle emphasizes the importance of acting in the best interest of the patient, striving to maximize their well-being and promote their recovery. Healthcare professionals must make decisions and recommendations that are guided by their professional knowledge and expertise, aiming to provide the highest quality of care possible.

Another essential ethical principle is that of non-maleficence, which emphasizes the duty to do no harm. Healthcare providers must take all necessary precautions to prevent harm and minimize risks to their patients. This includes providing accurate information, obtaining informed consent, and ensuring that treatments and interventions are safe and effective.

Autonomy and respect for patient autonomy is another crucial ethical obligation of healthcare providers. Patients have the right to make decisions about their own healthcare, including the right to refuse or choose certain treatments. Healthcare professionals must respect these choices and provide patients with the necessary information and support to make informed decisions about their care.

Furthermore, healthcare providers have an obligation to maintain patient confidentiality. Confidentiality is the cornerstone of trust in the healthcare relationship and ensures that patients feel safe and comfortable sharing sensitive information with their healthcare providers. Healthcare professionals must adhere to strict confidentiality standards, ensuring that patient information is protected and disclosed only when necessary and with the patient's consent.

Lastly, healthcare providers have a broader ethical obligation to advocate for justice and fairness in healthcare. This includes addressing disparities in access to healthcare, advocating for equitable distribution of resources, and challenging discriminatory practices. Healthcare professionals must strive to ensure that all patients receive equal and fair treatment, regardless of their background or socioeconomic status.

In conclusion, the ethical obligations of healthcare providers are multifaceted and require a delicate balance between the needs and rights of the patient, professional expertise, and societal considerations. Upholding these ethical principles is crucial for maintaining the trust and integrity of the healthcare profession. By prioritizing the principles of beneficence, non-maleficence, autonomy, confidentiality, and justice, healthcare providers can navigate the complex ethical terrain of medical dilemmas and ensure the best possible care for their patients.

Conflicts of Interest and Ethical Decision Making

In our complex and interconnected world, conflicts of interest are an unavoidable reality. They arise when individuals or organizations find themselves torn between their personal interests and their professional duties, leading to ethical dilemmas that can have profound implications for society. In the realm of healthcare and medicine, conflicts of interest pose particularly challenging ethical questions that demand careful consideration and thoughtful decision-making.

Medical professionals, from doctors to pharmaceutical researchers, often find themselves navigating an intricate web of conflicting interests. On one hand, they are driven by their commitment to the well-being of their patients and the advancement of medical science. On the other, they may face pressures from financial incentives, personal relationships, or industry affiliations that can cloud their judgment and compromise their ethical integrity.

Recognizing and addressing conflicts of interest is essential to maintaining trust and upholding the highest ethical standards in healthcare. It is crucial for medical professionals to be transparent about any potential conflicts, ensuring that their decision-making is guided by the best interests of their patients and the wider community.

Ethical decision-making in the face of conflicts of interest requires a robust framework that takes into account the principles of beneficence, autonomy, and justice. The concept of beneficence reminds us of the paramount importance of promoting the well-being of patients. Autonomy, on the other hand, underscores the significance of respecting patients' rights to make informed decisions about their own healthcare. Lastly, justice demands that medical professionals consider the fair distribution of resources and the equitable treatment of all patients, regardless of their social or economic backgrounds.

However, navigating conflicts of interest is not solely the responsibility of medical professionals. Patients and the public also have a role to play. By educating themselves about potential conflicts and advocating for transparency and accountability, individuals can actively contribute to a culture of ethical decision-making in healthcare.

In this subchapter, we will explore numerous real-life case studies that highlight the complexities of conflicts of interest in medicine. Through these stories, we will delve into the ethical considerations and decision-making processes involved, shedding light on the consequences of both sound and compromised ethical judgment. By deepening our understanding of conflicts of interest and ethical decision-making, we can collectively work towards a healthcare system that prioritizes patient welfare and upholds the highest ethical standards.

Whether you are a healthcare professional, a patient, or simply someone interested in ethics, this subchapter will provide valuable insights and thought-provoking discussions. Join us as we explore the intricate world of conflicts of interest and embark on a journey towards ethical decision-making in the realm of life and death.

Medical Errors and Accountability

In the realm of healthcare, medical errors are an unfortunate reality that can have profound consequences for patients and healthcare professionals alike. These errors, defined as preventable mistakes in healthcare delivery, can range from misdiagnosis and medication errors to surgical mistakes and communication breakdowns. While it is impossible to completely eradicate errors from healthcare, it is essential to establish a robust system of accountability to minimize their occurrence and mitigate their impact.

At the heart of addressing medical errors lies the ethical principle of accountability. Accountability ensures that healthcare professionals take responsibility for their actions and are transparent about any mistakes made. It is essential for maintaining public trust in the healthcare system and fostering a culture of safety and learning.

For patients, accountability means having access to accurate information about their healthcare providers' track record and the outcomes of their treatments. This transparency allows patients to make informed choices about their care and empowers them to actively participate in their healthcare decisions. It also enables patients to hold healthcare providers accountable for any errors or substandard care they may have received.

From a healthcare professional's perspective, accountability involves acknowledging errors, learning from them, and implementing strategies to prevent future mistakes. It requires an environment where healthcare professionals feel safe to report errors without fear of retribution, allowing for a thorough investigation and analysis of the root causes. By identifying the underlying factors contributing to errors, healthcare organizations can implement systemic changes and develop best practices to minimize risks.

In addition to individual accountability, there is a broader need for accountability within the healthcare system as a whole. This includes regulatory bodies, healthcare institutions, and policymakers. These entities play a crucial role in setting standards, enforcing regulations, and creating a culture of safety. Holding them accountable ensures that they prioritize patient well-being and actively work towards preventing medical errors.

Addressing medical errors and promoting accountability requires a multifaceted approach. It involves implementing robust reporting systems, fostering a culture of safety, providing education and training, and establishing effective communication channels between healthcare professionals and patients. It also necessitates ongoing research and collaboration to identify and implement evidence-based strategies to minimize errors.

By emphasizing accountability in healthcare, we can strive towards a system that values transparency, learning, and continuous improvement. This not only benefits patients but also empowers healthcare professionals to provide the best possible care while reducing the occurrence of preventable errors. Ultimately, by addressing medical errors and promoting accountability, we can work towards a safer and more ethical healthcare system for everyone.

Chapter 10: Ethical Dilemmas in Medical Practice

The Trolley Problem: Ethical Decision Making

Introduction:

In the pursuit of understanding complex ethical dilemmas, few scenarios are as thought-provoking and controversial as the Trolley Problem. This classic moral quandary challenges our intuitive sense of right and wrong, forcing us to question the ethics behind our decision-making. Examining this problem is crucial for anyone interested in the field of ethics, as it provides a framework for analyzing and discussing moral choices in various contexts.

Understanding the Trolley Problem:

The Trolley Problem presents a hypothetical situation where a runaway trolley is hurtling down a track, and you have the power to divert it onto another track. However, on the alternate track, there is a single individual who would be harmed or killed. The dilemma arises when you have to decide whether to take action and sacrifice one life to save the lives of several others.

Ethical Considerations:

The Trolley Problem serves as a catalyst for exploring the underlying principles that guide our ethical decision-making. It highlights conflicting moral theories, such as utilitarianism and deontology. Utilitarianism suggests that the morally right action is the one that maximizes overall happiness or minimizes overall harm. In this case, diverting the trolley to save more lives aligns with utilitarian thinking. On the other hand, deontological ethics emphasizes the importance of adhering to moral rules and duties. In this context, intentionally causing harm to an innocent person goes against deontological principles.

Real-World Applications:

While the Trolley Problem may seem like a theoretical exercise, its implications extend far beyond philosophy classrooms. This ethical dilemma can be applied to various real-world scenarios, including medical decision-making, autonomous vehicle programming, and even military operations. Exploring these applications allows us to grapple with the ethical complexities of life and death situations and encourages us to consider the broader impact of our choices.

Conclusion:

The Trolley Problem serves as a powerful tool for examining the intricacies of ethical decision-making. By delving into this thought experiment, we develop a deeper understanding of the underlying principles that guide our moral compass. Whether you are interested in ethics as an academic discipline or simply seeking to enhance your ethical reasoning skills, the Trolley Problem is an essential concept to explore. It challenges us to critically evaluate our beliefs, confront our biases, and ultimately strive for a more ethical society.

Withholding vs. Withdrawing Treatment: Ethical Considerations

In the realm of medical ethics, one topic that often sparks intense debates and ethical considerations is the decision to withhold or withdraw treatment. These decisions can arise in various medical scenarios, from end-of-life care to critical situations where the potential benefits of treatment are uncertain. Understanding the ethical implications of withholding or withdrawing treatment is crucial for both healthcare professionals and the general public.

When faced with such decisions, it is essential to consider the principles of autonomy, beneficence, non-maleficence, and justice. Autonomy refers to an individual's right to make independent decisions about their own healthcare. Beneficence emphasizes the duty to act in the best interest of the patient, while non-maleficence emphasizes the obligation to do no harm. Justice requires that healthcare resources be allocated fairly and equitably.

The decision to withhold treatment occurs when medical professionals, in consultation with the patient or their surrogate, choose not to initiate a particular treatment. This decision is often based on the belief that the treatment will not be effective or will impose undue burden on the patient. Withdrawing treatment, on the other hand, involves discontinuing a treatment that is already being administered. This decision is typically made when the treatment is no longer providing any benefit or is causing more harm than good.

In these complex ethical situations, healthcare professionals must carefully balance the principles mentioned above. They must consider the patient's values, wishes, and prognosis, along with the potential benefits and risks of the treatment. Communication with the patient or their surrogate is vital, ensuring that they understand the situation and the reasons behind the decision.

From an ethical standpoint, withholding or withdrawing treatment is not equivalent to euthanasia or physician-assisted suicide. These decisions aim to respect the patient's autonomy and ensure the best possible care while avoiding unnecessary suffering. However, it is crucial to acknowledge the emotional and psychological toll these decisions can have on patients, families, and healthcare providers. Supportive care, including pain management and emotional support, should be prioritized to alleviate any distress.

Ethical considerations surrounding the withholding or withdrawing of treatment are complex and multifaceted. They require a comprehensive understanding of the patient's medical condition, prognosis, and values. By engaging in open and compassionate discussions, healthcare providers can navigate these difficult decisions while upholding the principles of medical ethics and ensuring the best possible care for their patients.

Resource Allocation in Times of Crisis

In times of crisis, such as natural disasters or pandemics, the allocation of limited resources becomes an ethical quandary. The decisions made during these trying times can have profound consequences on individuals and communities. This subchapter delves into the complexities of resource allocation during emergencies, offering an ethical perspective on the matter.

When faced with limited resources, difficult decisions must be made regarding who receives medical treatment and support. These decisions should be based on ethical principles that prioritize the greatest good for the greatest number of people. However, determining what constitutes the "greatest good" is a complex task that requires careful consideration.

One ethical framework that can guide resource allocation is utilitarianism, which argues that actions should be aimed at maximizing overall happiness or well-being. In the context of crisis, this means allocating resources to those individuals who are most likely to benefit from them, with the aim of saving the most lives or reducing suffering as much as possible.

However, the utilitarian approach must be balanced with other ethical considerations, such as fairness and justice. It is crucial to avoid discriminating against certain individuals or groups based on irrelevant factors like race, gender, or social status. Fairness can be achieved by implementing transparent and unbiased decision-making processes, ensuring that all individuals have an equal chance of receiving the necessary resources.

Another ethical consideration is the duty to care for vulnerable populations. In times of crisis, it is essential to prioritize the needs of those who are most at risk, such as the elderly, children, and individuals with pre-existing health conditions. This requires a compassionate and empathetic approach, recognizing the inherent value and dignity of every human life.

Furthermore, it is important to engage in open and honest communication with the public about the resource allocation process. Transparency helps build trust and understanding among the affected community, even in the face of difficult decisions. By involving the public in the decision-making process, their voices can be heard, and their concerns can be addressed, fostering a sense of shared responsibility.

In conclusion, resource allocation in times of crisis is an ethical dilemma that requires careful consideration of utilitarian principles, fairness, justice, and the duty to care for vulnerable populations. By approaching resource allocation with compassion, transparency, and inclusivity, we can strive to make decisions that prioritize the well-being of the greatest number of people while upholding ethical standards.

Cultural and Religious Perspectives on Medical Ethics

In the complex and ever-evolving field of medical ethics, it is crucial to explore the diverse cultural and religious perspectives that shape our understanding of life and death. This subchapter delves into the intricate relationship between ethics, culture, and religion, shedding light on how these factors influence medical decision-making.

Culture plays a pivotal role in shaping our values, beliefs, and customs, which in turn influence our ethical perspectives. Every culture has its unique perspectives on life and death, with varying views on topics such as euthanasia, abortion, and organ transplantation. By understanding and respecting these cultural differences, healthcare professionals can provide more culturally sensitive care, ensuring that patients' values and beliefs are considered when making ethical decisions.

Religion, too, holds significant sway over medical ethics. The major world religions, such as Christianity, Islam, Judaism, Hinduism, and Buddhism, provide moral frameworks that guide believers in navigating medical dilemmas. For instance, some religions may promote the sanctity of life, prohibiting practices such as euthanasia or abortion, while others may emphasize the importance of compassion and relieving suffering.

Examining different religious perspectives on medical ethics can foster a deeper understanding of the diverse moral values held by individuals within a society. This knowledge enables healthcare professionals to provide compassionate care that respects and accommodates the religious beliefs of their patients.

Moreover, cultural and religious perspectives on medical ethics often intersect, creating a rich tapestry of ethical considerations. For instance, in some cultures, the family unit holds great importance, and decisions regarding end-of-life care may involve the input of the entire family. Religious beliefs, such as the belief in an afterlife, can also greatly influence an individual's decisions about medical interventions or the withdrawal of life-sustaining treatments.

By examining cultural and religious perspectives on medical ethics, we can foster a more inclusive and empathetic healthcare system. It is crucial for healthcare professionals and policymakers to be knowledgeable about these perspectives and ensure that ethical guidelines and policies reflect the values of the diverse populations they serve.

In conclusion, culture and religion are two vital lenses through which we can understand and navigate the complexities of medical ethics. By appreciating the diverse cultural and religious perspectives that shape our understanding of life and death, we can provide ethical and compassionate care that respects the values and beliefs of all individuals. This subchapter serves as a stepping stone towards a more inclusive and culturally sensitive healthcare system, emphasizing the importance of understanding the ethical implications of cultural and religious perspectives in medical decision-making.

Chapter 11: Ethical Frameworks and Resolving Medical Dilemmas

Utilitarianism and its Application in Medical Ethics

In the realm of medical ethics, one ethical theory that holds significant relevance is utilitarianism. Utilitarianism is a consequentialist ethical framework that focuses on maximizing overall well-being and happiness for the greatest number of people. This subchapter explores the fundamental principles of utilitarianism and its application in various medical dilemmas.

At its core, utilitarianism emphasizes the notion of utility, which refers to the net balance of pleasure over pain. According to this theory, the morally right action is the one that produces the greatest amount of overall happiness, even if it may involve sacrificing the interests of a few individuals for the greater good of the majority.

In the context of medical ethics, utilitarianism helps guide decision-making processes that involve difficult choices, such as resource allocation, end-of-life care, and organ transplantation. For example, when faced with limited medical resources, utilitarianism suggests that the resources should be allocated to those who would benefit the most, thereby maximizing overall well-being.

Utilitarianism also plays a crucial role in end-of-life care decisions, particularly in situations where patients are unable to express their wishes. In such cases, medical professionals often rely on the principle of beneficence, which aligns with utilitarianism, to make decisions that prioritize the patient's best interests and overall happiness.

Furthermore, utilitarianism provides a framework for ethical considerations in organ transplantation. It supports the idea of maximizing the number of lives saved and improved through organ donation, even if it means sacrificing the interests of the deceased or their families. Utilitarianism urges the prioritization of the greater good over individual preferences.

However, utilitarianism is not without its criticisms. Some argue that it can lead to the violation of individual rights and the neglect of minority interests. It may also face challenges in accurately quantifying and comparing different types of happiness or well-being.

Despite these criticisms, utilitarianism remains a significant ethical theory in medical ethics, providing a valuable perspective on decision-making processes. By focusing on overall happiness and well-being, utilitarianism helps navigate complex medical dilemmas and encourages a broader perspective that takes into account the interests of the many.

In conclusion, utilitarianism offers a consequentialist approach to medical ethics, emphasizing the maximization of overall happiness and well-being. Its application in medical dilemmas provides a framework for decision-making processes, particularly in areas such as resource allocation, end-of-life care, and organ transplantation. While it is not without its criticisms, utilitarianism offers valuable insights into ethical considerations in medicine and enables a balanced approach that prioritizes the greater good.

Deontology: Duty-based Ethics in Medical Practice

In the realm of medical ethics, one prominent ethical framework that guides healthcare professionals is deontology. Derived from the Greek word "deon," meaning duty or obligation, deontology emphasizes the importance of adhering to moral principles and fulfilling one's obligations, regardless of the consequences. This subchapter explores the application of deontological principles in medical practice, shedding light on the ethical dilemmas faced by healthcare professionals and the role of duty-based ethics in resolving them.

When it comes to medical decision-making, deontology places the utmost importance on the ethical duties and responsibilities of healthcare providers. This approach emphasizes the inherent value of human life and the moral duty to prioritize the well-being and autonomy of patients. It recognizes that ethical decisions should not be based solely on the outcomes or consequences but on the principles that underpin them.

Within the realm of medical practice, deontology helps guide decisions related to informed consent, patient confidentiality, and end-of-life care, among others. Healthcare professionals are obligated to provide patients with accurate and complete information about their conditions and treatment options, allowing them to make informed decisions about their own healthcare. This adherence to truth-telling reflects the deontological principle of respecting patient autonomy.

Moreover, deontology establishes a duty for healthcare providers to maintain patient confidentiality. This principle recognizes that patients have a right to privacy and that trust is essential for effective medical care. Healthcare professionals must resist the temptation to breach patient confidentiality, even if divulging information could potentially benefit others. The duty to respect patient privacy takes precedence over other considerations.

Deontological ethics also plays a crucial role in end-of-life care, particularly in the context of medical interventions that may prolong suffering without offering a reasonable chance of recovery. In such cases, deontology supports the ethical duty of healthcare professionals to prioritize the well-being and dignity of the patient, even if it means refraining from pursuing aggressive treatments. This principle aligns with the concept of "do no harm" and upholds the sanctity of life.

In conclusion, deontology serves as a guiding framework in medical practice, helping healthcare professionals navigate complex ethical dilemmas. By prioritizing moral duties and obligations, deontological ethics ensures that healthcare decisions are grounded in principles that respect patient autonomy, maintain confidentiality, and prioritize the well-being and dignity of individuals. Understanding and applying these duty-based ethics in medical practice is crucial for delivering ethical and compassionate care to patients.

Virtue Ethics and its Relevance in Healthcare

Ethics plays a crucial role in every aspect of our lives, and healthcare is no exception. When it comes to making decisions about life and death, it becomes even more critical to have a solid ethical framework. One such framework that holds immense relevance in healthcare is virtue ethics.

Virtue ethics focuses on the character and moral virtues of individuals, rather than on strict rules or consequences. It emphasizes developing virtuous qualities such as compassion, honesty, integrity, and empathy. In the context of healthcare, virtue ethics provides a strong foundation for guiding ethical decision-making and promoting the well-being of patients.

In the realm of medicine, healthcare professionals are entrusted with the responsibility of caring for the sick and vulnerable. Virtue ethics emphasizes the importance of cultivating virtues that enable healthcare practitioners to provide the highest level of care. Compassion, for instance, allows doctors and nurses to empathize with their patients and provide comfort during times of distress. Honesty and integrity, on the other hand, ensure open and transparent communication with patients, fostering trust and mutual respect.

Virtue ethics also guides healthcare professionals in their everyday interactions with colleagues and the larger healthcare system. It encourages collaboration, respect, and professionalism within the healthcare team, ultimately improving patient outcomes. By prioritizing virtues such as fairness, justice, and accountability, healthcare practitioners can navigate complex ethical dilemmas with integrity and make decisions that promote the best interests of their patients.

Moreover, virtue ethics extends beyond the realm of individual healthcare professionals and applies to the healthcare system as a whole. It calls for institutions to prioritize virtues such as compassion, equity, and patient-centeredness to ensure the provision of high-quality and ethical care. By embracing these virtues, healthcare institutions can create an environment that promotes holistic well-being and respects the dignity of every patient.

In conclusion, virtue ethics offers a valuable framework for addressing ethical issues in healthcare. By focusing on the development of virtuous qualities, healthcare professionals can cultivate the necessary character traits to provide compassionate and ethical care. Moreover, virtue ethics guides the interactions between healthcare professionals and the larger healthcare system, fostering collaboration and prioritizing the well-being of patients. As we navigate the complexities of medical dilemmas, virtue ethics serves as a moral compass, ensuring that ethics remains at the heart of healthcare.

Principles-Based Approach to Ethical Decision Making

Ethical decision making is an essential aspect of our lives, especially when it comes to medical dilemmas that involve matters of life and death. In this subchapter, we will explore the principles-based approach to ethical decision making, which provides a structured framework to navigate complex ethical situations. This approach is particularly relevant in the field of healthcare, where professionals often face difficult choices that can have profound impacts on patients and their families.

At its core, the principles-based approach to ethical decision making relies on four primary principles: autonomy, beneficence, non-maleficence, and justice. These principles serve as a guide to help individuals evaluate the ethical implications of their actions and make morally sound choices.

Autonomy emphasizes the importance of respecting an individual's right to make decisions regarding their own healthcare. It recognizes that patients have the right to be informed, provide informed consent, and actively participate in the decision-making process. This principle places a significant emphasis on patient-centered care, ensuring that their preferences and values are taken into account.

Beneficence focuses on promoting the well-being and best interests of the patient. Healthcare professionals must act in a manner that maximizes the benefits for the patient, striving to achieve the best possible outcome while considering the individual's unique circumstances. This principle encourages healthcare providers to act with compassion, empathy, and a genuine desire to improve the patient's health and quality of life.

Non-maleficence, on the other hand, emphasizes the importance of avoiding harm to the patient. Healthcare professionals must carefully assess the potential risks associated with their actions and strive to minimize any potential harm. This principle serves as a reminder that the primary goal of healthcare is to do no harm, even if it means refraining from certain interventions or treatments.

Lastly, justice focuses on the fair distribution of healthcare resources and the equitable treatment of all individuals. This principle acknowledges the need for healthcare systems to prioritize the needs of all patients, regardless of their social or economic status. It calls for ethical decision making to be guided by fairness, impartiality, and equal access to healthcare services.

By applying these principles to ethical decision making, healthcare professionals, patients, and their families can navigate complex medical dilemmas with greater clarity and integrity. The principles-based approach provides a solid foundation for ethical deliberation, ensuring that decisions are grounded in respect for autonomy, the pursuit of beneficence, the avoidance of harm, and the promotion of justice.

In conclusion, ethical decision making is a critical skill that is particularly relevant in the field of healthcare. The principles-based approach provides a structured framework to guide individuals in navigating complex ethical dilemmas. By considering the principles of autonomy, beneficence, non-maleficence, and justice, healthcare professionals can make morally sound decisions that prioritize the well-being and best interests of patients. This approach highlights the importance of patient-centered care, avoiding harm, and ensuring equitable access to healthcare resources. By understanding and applying the principles-based approach to ethical decision making, we can contribute to a more ethical and compassionate healthcare system for everyone.

Chapter 12: Conclusion and Future Directions in Medical Ethics

Recapitulation of Key Ethical Issues Explored

In this subchapter, we will provide a concise recapitulation of the key ethical issues that have been explored throughout the book, "The Ethics of Life and Death: Exploring Medical Dilemmas." This book delves into the complex and thought-provoking field of medical ethics, aiming to provide a comprehensive understanding of the ethical dilemmas faced within the realm of healthcare.

One of the primary ethical issues discussed in this book is the concept of autonomy and informed consent. The right of patients to make decisions about their own healthcare, including the right to refuse treatment, is a fundamental principle of medical ethics. However, conflicts may arise when patients lack decision-making capacity or when their choices may lead to harm. The book explores the delicate balance between respecting autonomy and ensuring the best possible outcomes for patients.

Another significant ethical concern examined is the allocation of scarce resources. With limited resources and a growing population, healthcare professionals often face difficult decisions regarding who should receive certain treatments or interventions. This book delves into the ethical principles that guide resource allocation, such as fairness, need, and utility. It also critically examines the potential biases and challenges that arise in this process.

The sensitive topics of euthanasia and physician-assisted suicide are thoroughly explored within the pages of this book. The ethical dilemmas surrounding end-of-life care and the right to die with dignity are complex and highly controversial. The book provides a nuanced discussion of the arguments for and against these practices, considering the moral, legal, and societal implications involved.

Additionally, the book delves into the ethical considerations surrounding reproductive technologies, genetic engineering, and organ transplantation. These advancements in medical science have raised profound ethical questions about the limits of human intervention and the potential consequences for society. The ethical implications of these medical dilemmas are examined from various perspectives, providing readers with a comprehensive understanding of the complexities involved.

Overall, "The Ethics of Life and Death: Exploring Medical Dilemmas" offers a comprehensive exploration of key ethical issues within the field of healthcare. It addresses these issues with the aim of stimulating critical thinking and fostering a deeper understanding of the ethical challenges faced by healthcare professionals, policymakers, and society as a whole. This book is a valuable resource for anyone interested in ethics, medical ethics, or the broader implications of medical decision-making.

The Evolving Landscape of Medical Ethics

Medical ethics is a field that is constantly evolving, shaped by advancements in medical technology, changing social norms, and the ever-growing complexities of medical dilemmas. This subchapter delves into the intricacies of this fascinating subject, addressing the ethical considerations that arise in the realm of healthcare and exploring the ongoing evolution of medical ethics.

In today's world, medical ethics is a concern that transcends professional boundaries. It is no longer just the domain of healthcare providers; it is a topic that affects each and every one of us. Whether we are patients, caregivers, or simply members of society, we are all stakeholders in the ethical dimensions of healthcare. Understanding the evolving landscape of medical ethics is crucial for making informed decisions and participating in discussions that shape the future of healthcare.

One of the key factors driving the evolution of medical ethics is the rapid advancement of medical technology. Innovations such as genetic testing, artificial intelligence, and precision medicine present new ethical challenges that require careful consideration. For example, the ability to manipulate genes raises questions about the limits of human intervention in the natural course of life. As these technologies become more prevalent, we must grapple with ethical dilemmas surrounding their use and implications for society.

Moreover, changing social norms and values have a significant impact on medical ethics. Issues such as patient autonomy, end-of-life care, and reproductive rights have become increasingly prominent in public discourse. The evolving understanding of individual rights and the concept of personhood further complicate ethical decision-making in medical contexts. As society becomes more diverse and inclusive, medical ethics must adapt to accommodate different cultural, religious, and philosophical perspectives.

Another pivotal aspect of the evolving landscape of medical ethics is the growing recognition of the importance of interdisciplinary collaboration. Ethical decision-making in healthcare requires input from professionals with diverse backgrounds, including physicians, nurses, philosophers, theologians, and policymakers. This interdisciplinary approach allows for a more comprehensive understanding of the ethical implications of medical practices and facilitates the development of guidelines and policies that promote the well-being of patients and society as a whole.

In conclusion, the field of medical ethics is constantly evolving, shaped by advancements in medical technology, changing social norms, and the need for interdisciplinary collaboration. As members of society, we all have a stake in understanding and participating in discussions about medical ethics. By exploring the evolving landscape of medical ethics, we can navigate the complex ethical dilemmas that arise in healthcare, ensure the protection of individual rights, and contribute to the development of ethical guidelines that promote the well-being of all.

The Role of Education and Training in Ethical Decision Making

Ethics play a crucial role in every aspect of our lives, and in no area is it more evident than in the field of medicine. Healthcare professionals are constantly faced with complex moral dilemmas that require them to make difficult decisions. These decisions can have profound implications for the well-being and even the lives of their patients. In order to navigate these ethical challenges successfully, education and training in ethical decision making are of paramount importance.

Education and training in ethics provide healthcare professionals with the necessary tools and knowledge to make informed decisions that are rooted in moral principles. By learning about different ethical theories and frameworks, professionals can develop a solid understanding of the ethical considerations involved in medical decision making. They can also gain insight into the values and beliefs that underpin these considerations. This knowledge is essential for healthcare professionals to make ethical decisions that align with their professional responsibilities and provide the best possible care for their patients.

Furthermore, education and training in ethics help healthcare professionals develop critical thinking skills. They learn how to analyze complex situations, consider multiple perspectives, and evaluate the potential consequences of their actions. These skills enable them to make well-reasoned and morally justifiable decisions when faced with ethical dilemmas. By engaging in case studies, discussions, and simulations, professionals can practice applying ethical principles to real-life scenarios, thereby honing their decision-making abilities.

Education and training also foster empathy and compassion in healthcare professionals. By understanding the ethical implications of their actions, they can better appreciate the impact these decisions have on their patients. This awareness allows them to provide patient-centered care that respects individual autonomy and promotes the well-being of their patients.

Moreover, education and training in ethics help healthcare professionals develop the courage to make difficult decisions. Ethical dilemmas often involve weighing conflicting principles and making choices that may be unpopular or controversial. Education and training instill the confidence to act in accordance with one's moral convictions, even in the face of adversity or opposition.

In conclusion, education and training in ethical decision making are vital for healthcare professionals to navigate the complex ethical challenges they encounter. By providing knowledge, critical thinking skills, empathy, and courage, these educational efforts empower professionals to make morally sound decisions that prioritize the well-being and autonomy of their patients. As society continues to progress, it is imperative that ethical education remains a priority to ensure that healthcare professionals uphold the highest ethical standards in their practice.

Challenges and Opportunities in Advancing Medical Ethics

Introduction:

In the ever-evolving field of medicine, ethical considerations play a crucial role in ensuring the well-being and dignity of patients. As our understanding of medical science expands and technology advances, new challenges arise in the realm of medical ethics. This subchapter explores the key challenges and opportunities that lie ahead in advancing medical ethics, and how they impact not only healthcare professionals but also every individual.

1. Rapid Technological Advancements:

One of the major challenges in medical ethics is keeping pace with the rapid advancements in technology. Innovations such as genetic engineering, artificial intelligence, and telemedicine raise critical questions about patient autonomy, privacy, and the potential for discrimination. Healthcare professionals and policymakers must navigate these ethical dilemmas to ensure that technology is used ethically and responsibly for the benefit of all.

2. Access to Healthcare:

Ethical issues surrounding access to healthcare remain a significant challenge in many parts of the world. Disparities in healthcare resources and affordability, particularly in low-income communities, pose ethical questions about distributive justice and the right to healthcare. Addressing these challenges requires a collective effort from governments, healthcare providers, and society at large to ensure equitable access to quality healthcare for everyone.

3. End-of-Life Care:

Advancements in medical technology have also raised complex ethical questions about end-of-life care. The debate surrounding euthanasia, physician-assisted suicide, and palliative care continues to be a topic of contention. Balancing patient autonomy, quality of life, and the preservation of life itself presents a challenging ethical landscape that requires thoughtful and compassionate decision-making.

4. Informed Consent and Privacy:

The digital age has brought forth new ethical challenges regarding informed consent and patient privacy. With the widespread adoption of electronic health records and data-sharing platforms, the protection of patient information and the respect for individual autonomy become paramount. Striking the right balance between the benefits of sharing medical data for research and the protection of patient privacy is a challenge that must be navigated ethically.

Opportunities:

While challenges exist, there are also numerous opportunities to advance medical ethics:

1. Education and Training:

Increasing awareness about medical ethics and providing comprehensive training to healthcare professionals can empower them to navigate ethical dilemmas effectively. Ethical education should be integrated into medical curricula to create a culture that values ethical decision-making.

2. Collaboration and Dialogue:

Opportunities for collaboration and dialogue between healthcare professionals, patients, policymakers, and ethicists can lead to the development of ethical guidelines and policies that reflect diverse perspectives and protect patient rights.

3. Research and Innovation:

Advancements in medical ethics can be achieved through dedicated research in the field. By studying ethical issues and their impact on patient outcomes, researchers can contribute to the development of evidence-based guidelines and best practices.

Conclusion:

Advancing medical ethics is essential for ensuring the highest standards of patient care and protecting individual rights. By acknowledging the challenges and embracing the opportunities, we can collectively work towards a future where medical ethics are at the forefront of healthcare decisions. This subchapter aims to inspire individuals from all walks of life to engage in ethical discourse and contribute to the advancement of medical ethics for the betterment of society as a whole.